The Return of the Feminine
&
the World Soul

Endorsements

This book has been deliberately shared with men and women of all walks of life and different parts of the world. Here are some of their responses, kept in their entirety. They belong to the story of life reclaiming its mystery.

"Llewellyn Vaughan-Lee presents us with a clear picture of the Feminine which is now essential to building a new vision and value for our dear planet earth."

—MARION WOODMAN, PH.D., JUNGIAN ANALYST AND AUTHOR

"... taps into what may be the most important message of our time—the need for the re-emergence of the feminine. As he so beautifully recounts, only through the Divine Feminine can the world, now so desperately wounded and degraded, begin to heal and transform itself. Llewellyn Vaughan-Lee explains what our role is in this process, how we can bring the masculine and feminine into greater balance and bridge the unreal divide between spirit and matter. It is a collective enterprise, and we all must be engaged in restoring the feminine to her rightful place. Llewellyn's narrative explains so much of what we intuitively know but what so few can articulate as well.... One of the most inspiring spiritual books of our day and a must read for all those seeking to understand the global transformation now underway."

—DENA MERRIAM, FOUNDER AND CONVENER OF
THE GLOBAL PEACE INITIATIVE FOR WOMEN

"... the sort of book that offers its readers new eyes. Vaughan-Lee's profound yet easily accessible exposition of the Divine Feminine will appeal to anyone who yearns for greater wholeness in life. A beautiful formula for the healing of a world which has developed masculine principle competency to the point of self extinction."

—RACHEL NAOMI REMEN, M.D., AUTHOR OF *Kitchen Table Wisdom*
AND *My Grandfather's Blessings*; CLINICAL PROFESSOR OF FAMILY AND
COMMUNITY MEDICINE AT UNIVERSITY OF CALIFORNIA SF SCHOOL OF
MEDICINE, AND FOUNDER AND DIRECTOR OF THE INSTITUTE FOR
THE STUDY OF HEALTH AND ILLNESS AT COMMONWEAL

"This beautiful book celebrates our interconnectedness in Her eternal web of life."

—MEINRAD CRAIGHEAD, ARTIST, SCHOLAR, AND VISIONARY

"This book is very perceptive, deeply moving and calling us all to attention! We have lived long in a world dominated by the role of the masculine consciousness—trenchant, linear, centered in acquisition.... The divine feminine is that ocean of a 'transforming power' that can turn into gold the mixed alloy of humanity, it is time to come forward into the arena of the world's life—and play a part. Sri Aurobindo, the great visionary of modern India, rightly says, 'It is only the woman who can link the new world with the old.'"

—ASTER PATEL, GOVERNING BOARD, AUROVILLE, INDIA

"This book contains an important message for our time. It is an inspirational text to awaken the reader to the alchemical mystery of the Soul of the World (*Anima Mundi*)—an important aspect of the Divine Feminine and the mysteries of Sophia. This alive and accessible work deserves a wide readership."

—ROBERT POWELL, PH.D., CO-FOUNDER OF THE SOPHIA FOUNDATION OF NORTH AMERICA, AUTHOR *The Sophia Teachings* (BOOK AND TAPES) AND *The Mystery, Biography, and Destiny of Mary Magdalene*

"If being of service to Life—to our beloved, wounded planet and all creation—is the central task of our time, this book is a lighthouse on that journey. It is a luminous, wise, inspiring and generous book, magical and serene. An invitation into, and open door toward, a new way of being, lived in true collaboration and interconnectedness with the Oneness of all Life. Reading this gives an experience of remembrance, redemption, direction, and renewal—a kind of north star for our souls. I couldn't recommend it more highly and will carry it as a compass, with gratitude, to help guide the way ahead."

—JENEPHER STOWELL, DIRECTOR, RETREAT CENTER, COMMONWEAL

"… shares with us a key to our times. In this book he says that in order to return to balance we must reclaim ourselves and our relationship with the deep feminine. He reminds us that our First Nation Peoples have a way of life that is centered in the sacredness of life and the interconnectedness of it all. Our elders tell us that when the Mother of All Creation is fully present then all is in balance. It is time for us to call her home… and begin our dialogue with The First Grandmother that dreamed it all. As Grandmother Agnes, spokesperson for the International Council of Thirteen Indigenous Grandmothers, says, 'This is a time when we must take the most important journey of all—that fourteen inches from our head to our heart!!'"

—JYOTI, AMBASSADOR FOR THE INTERNATIONAL COUNCIL OF THIRTEEN INDIGENOUS GRANDMOTHERS, AND SPIRITUAL DIRECTOR OF THE CENTER FOR SACRED STUDIES

"In this profound work, I experienced scintillating beacons of light which my heart recognizes as the spiral of Oneness.... This is a guidebook as well as a celebration of remembering.... a guide to the secrets that we will want to know in our hearts as we embrace and transform energies of the shifts to come that include the difficult as well as the sublime."

—DR. MARJ BRITT, SENIOR MINISTER, UNITY OF TUSTIN, CALIFORNIA

"… these writings touch the essential commitment needed now to heal the feminine and move beyond patriarchal wounding without rancor or bitterness. Llewellyn Vaughan-Lee's voice calls to us both intimately and with forceful clarity to deeply engage in the nurturance of life. His message for women is a wake-up call..."

—MYOSHO VIRGINIA MATTHEWS, ZEN BUDDHIST NUN, MOTHER, DANCER

… continues at the back of the book …

The Return of the Feminine
&
the World Soul

*a collection of writings and
transcribed talks
by*

LLEWELLYN VAUGHAN-LEE

*gathered by Anat Vaughan-Lee
and Barbara Romanoff*

First published in the United States in 2009 by
The Golden Sufi Center
P.O. Box 456, Point Reyes, California 94956
www.goldensufi.org

Second printing 2011.

Cover design by Anat Vaughan-Lee.
Cover photo by Anthony Plummer, www.anthonyplummer.com.
©2009 Anthony Plummer.

ISBN 978-1-890350-14-7

Printed and Bound by Thompson-Shore, Inc.

Library of Congress Cataloging-in-Publication Data
Vaughan-Lee, Llewellyn.
  The return of the feminine & the world soul : a collection of
writings / by Llewellyn Vaughan-Lee.
      p. cm.
  Includes bibliographical references and index.
  ISBN 978-1-890350-14-7 (pbk. : alk. paper)
  1. Mysticism. 2. Femininity--Religious aspects. 3. Wisdom.
  4. Soul. I. Title. II. Title: Return of the feminine and the world soul.
  BL625.V385 2009
  297.4--dc22
                                        2009012028

Contents

"Then creation recognized its Creator in its own forms and appearances. For in the beginning, when God said, 'Let it be!' and it came to pass, the means and the Matrix of creation was Love, because all creation was formed through Her as in the twinkling of an eye."

THE HOLY SPIRIT AS
SAPIENTIA ST. HILDEGARD VON BINGEN

Foreword

I met Llewellyn Vaughan-Lee in 2005. Since then I have been following Llewellyn's writing on the divine feminine, and as a woman and a practitioner of shamanism, I find that his work speaks to my heart. I have found that although we have ridden different waves we tend to land on the same shore.

Indigenous teachings embrace the divine feminine in a way that is crucial for healing ourselves and the earth. For thousands of years it has been known that everything that exists in this world is alive and has a spirit. We are connected to a web of life that is impacted by the behavior of all that is alive. This ancient understanding of the divine feminine, the interconnected oneness of all creation, is a central theme in Llewellyn's writings. As he writes, when we speak to the soul of the trees, rocks, rivers, etc., we speak to the divine within creation.

In shamanism there is a practice that comes from different traditions called deep listening. Through deep listening we know how to avoid destroying the world once again. The answers lie in nature —nature is always sharing her teachings with us. The answers also lie in our own internal nature/inner wisdom. We must move the energy from our heads to our hearts. We must remember what we love about life and what brings us to a place of awe and wonder, reigniting our passion. We must remember how to honor and respect life with each breath, step, word, and thought. What you bless blesses you in return.

We can use the practice of deep inner listening to go beyond what our ordinary ears can hear, back into the reaches of the invisible, the feminine light and knowing, and the love that connects us all. To be of ultimate service to the planet we must reconnect to that innate feminine knowing that teaches us of the power of change that comes from being rather than doing.

In *The Return of the Feminine and the World Soul* Llewellyn addresses all these principles and more in a unique way. Llewellyn's gift in writing goes beyond a mere intellectual approach. His true gift is that he finds the words that go deep into your cells like a flower soaking up the life-giving light of the sun after a strong cleansing rain. In this way he creates the space beyond thinking, allowing you to come in contact with the forgotten and neglected place of that sacred knowing and to live the teachings.

I have read all of Llewellyn Vaughan-Lee's books and have been inspired by each one of them. In this book Llewellyn puts together his teachings on the feminine, which he stresses again and again is central in working with global healing and transformation and life's regeneration. In these writings he reminds us of the primal secrets of creation that belong to the feminine. He emphasizes how this deep knowledge is by nature an inseparable part of the woman's body and her inner knowing, and how it is especially needed in this time of great crisis to revitalize life as it is meant to be lived. He also reminds us of our ancient understanding of the *anima mundi,* the soul of the world, and how vital her presence is at this time. It is time for us to bring back the soul of the world by once again honoring this life-giving force.

I know everyone reading this book will be inspired. So please read on.

SANDRA INGERMAN
AUTHOR OF *Medicine for the Earth*
AND *How to Heal Toxic Thoughts*

The following introduction is essential for the reader to understand the reason for this compilation of materials, and its contribution at this moment in time.

Introduction

The assembly is filled with fragrance
at the mention of her,
and every tongue utters her name.
IBN 'ARABÎ[1]

The following chapters are a compilation of my writings on the feminine from 1991 until 2008. Over these years I have written, lectured, and given interviews on the subject of the feminine principle, the sacred feminine. My earliest writings concern my own experience of the feminine from a psychological perspective, the *anima* or soul figure within my own psyche as she expressed herself in dreams and images, her darkness and light, her power and beauty. From this inner reconnection with a feminine that has only too often been rejected, misunderstood and mistreated, I began to value and understand the role of the feminine on the spiritual quest, the importance of listening, receptivity, and sacred space that is needed for spiritual rebirth and living the longing of the soul.

These feminine qualities belong to both men and women, and they draw us into the depths within us, into the mysteries of the soul whose wisdom is called Sophia. They also reconnect us with the primal pain of the feminine that has been so abused by our masculine culture. We come to experience her tears and wounds, her pain which is also the pain of our own soul. In the realm of the feminine everything is connected, nothing is excluded. And working with people, especially women, listening to their dreams and stories, I began to see how this pain, this denial, is a wound in each of us that needs to be understood and forgiven if we are to reclaim our true spiritual heritage, the innate knowledge of the feminine and the wisdom of the earth.

My own journey took me beyond my individual quest into the drama of the whole, feeling the suffering of the earth and its longing to reawaken from this nightmare of exploitation and patriarchal greed. Here I experienced the pressing need to reclaim the wisdom and power of the Goddess, Her healing and transformative potential. And I glimpsed how this energy is especially present within women, and how women have a crucial role to play in redeeming the sacred feminine and learning once again how to work with her. Although the feminine is an important part of a man's psyche, women carry her wisdom and power in every cell of their body, and they have a responsibility in reawakening her potential.

In the story of our relationship to the earth I was drawn further, back to the ancient understanding of the *anima mundi*, the soul of the world, the divine principle within creation. Throughout history, in different times and cultures, there has been a relationship with the *anima mundi*, and ways to work with her, to bring her into daily life, particularly through art and the imagination. This feminine consciousness within all of life needs our attention in order to redeem our civilization and our world. Her cry needs to be heard, her knowing brought into our consciousness.

My own spiritual journey has followed the Sufi path of love, whose mysteries of the heart have always had a central place for the feminine. For the Sufi wayfarer it is love's feminine quality of longing that draws us back to our Beloved. The mystic lover waits in a deep space of feminine receptivity and unknowing for the Beloved to reveal Himself. This inner love affair of the soul with God has taught me much about the relationship with the feminine, and the Sufi tradition of images and mystical poetry has helped me to articulate some of her mystery. The fragrance of this tradition of lovers will be present in these pages.

Although this material comes from my own personal journey, I have stressed how the work of the feminine belongs to the healing and transformation of the whole. The book begins with chapters that focus on our need to revalue the feminine, to understand how she has a central part to play in the work of global healing and transformation. Her natural consciousness holds a deep understanding of the interconnections of life, how all the different parts relate together: how her awakening oneness can unfold. And every woman has in her spiritual centers the sacred substance of creation that is necessary for life's regeneration. Without the full participation of the feminine nothing new can be born. The reader is then taken into the dimension of the *anima mundi*, whose ancient wisdom and understanding of life's oneness is needed if the world is to be redeemed. I have included as an appendix a psychological and spiritual perspective on the feminine that began this exploration, how the journey to the soul of the world began with my own soul.

Part of the difficulty of understanding and describing the feminine is her very elusive nature, the veils that surround her, as well as our patriarchal repression and denial of her wisdom and power. Also the ancient feminine mysteries, her initiations and teachings, were never written down. She is not easily fixed and defined, but is mysterious in her continual movement and change. She belongs to the silvery light of the moon and its many reflections rather than the harsh glare of masculine sunshine and its rational constructs. She is more easily alluded to and hinted at, expressing the mystery and matrix of creation that is always a wonder rather than something to be explained. So these chapters do not attempt a rational, linear explanation of the feminine, but are more facets of a mirror reflecting different feminine qualities and ways of being. In this gathered material there are many repetitions, as each chapter treats a repeated theme from a slightly different perspective, and so over the whole book a more rounded and complete picture of the repeated theme subtly emerges. This is also part of the mystery of the feminine, whose creation is an eternal round of evolving repetition. Each moment the same divine wonder is expressed in a slightly different way.

Also repetition in itself has a value: after such a long time and such a deep conditioning of neglect and forgetting of the nature and quality and value of the feminine in our culture, there is a need to bring her back into consciousness. In a culture that is so steeped in masculine values as ours is, articulating these long-forgotten themes only once may not be enough. There is a need to emphasize her again and again until her qualities once again become part of our relationship to life. The more we are reminded of her, the better she will find a foothold again in our individual consciousness and in our collective culture.

The feminine belongs to the inner worlds as much as to the outer world of creation. She is part of the mystery of the soul, of the womb of the world. Our masculine culture has focused on an external, definable and measurable world, but the feminine knows a different dimension—what is hidden within, often in the darkness. Much of these writings belong to the inner worlds, which are traditionally the home of the mystic and shaman, the poet, the priestess, and the seer. These realms, often rich in symbols, feelings, and images, accessed through visions and the imagination, are not well known in our culture, and our language is ill equipped to describe them, just as our language itself belongs to a masculine, rational culture, one that likes things to be defined rather than just alluded to. In reading this book it is important to recognize the limitations of language, and allow what is beyond the words to speak to you.

Rather than explain the role of the feminine in a logical, linear manner, these chapters attempt to draw the reader into her wisdom and mystery. There is no single definition of the feminine, but there can be an awakening to her ways, to her qualities and powers. Sometimes I have called her "the divine," or "the Goddess" or "the feminine principle" or the *"anima mundi."* The feminine does not like to be caught in any single name or fixed explanation. She is a way of relating to life and to oneself and to the divine.

It is also important to remember that the divine feminine is not in any contrast or opposition to the masculine. Within her sacred wholeness everything is included. And when I refer to the unknowable aspect of the divine that is beyond all form or knowing as He, It has no gender: that "He" is not masculine as opposed to feminine. Although we may live in a culture dominated by separation, the divine is beyond any division. Yet the feminine has her own fragrance, her particular magic. Hopefully in these pages something of her true nature will come into consciousness. She will reveal some of her qualities, lift some of her veils.

*Because humanity has a central function
in the whole of creation, what we deny to ourself
we deny to all of life. In denying the feminine her sacred
power and purpose we have impoverished life in ways
we do not understand. We have denied life its sacred
source of meaning and divine purpose,
which was understood by the
ancient priestesses.*

— 1 —
Reclaiming the Feminine Mystery of Creation

*"Then creation recognized its Creator in its own forms
and appearances. For in the beginning, when God said, 'Let it be!'
and it came to pass, the means and the Matrix of creation
was Love, because all creation was formed through
Her as in the twinkling of an eye."*
THE HOLY SPIRIT AS SAPIENTIA ST. HILDEGARD VON BINGEN[1]

THE MATRIX OF CREATION

The feminine is the matrix of creation. This truth is something profound and elemental, and every woman knows it in the cells of her body, in her instinctual depths. Out of the substance of her very being life comes forth. She can conceive and give birth, participate in the greatest mystery of bringing a soul into life. And yet we have forgotten, or been denied, the depths of this mystery, of how the divine light of the soul creates a body in the womb of a woman, and how the mother shares in this wonder, giving her own blood, her own body, to what will be born. Our culture's focus on a disembodied, transcendent God has left women bereft, denying them the sacredness of this simple mystery of divine love.

What we do not realize is that this patriarchal denial affects not only every woman, but also life itself. When we deny the divine mystery of the feminine we also deny something fundamental to life. We separate life from its sacred core, from the matrix that nourishes all of creation. We cut our world off from the source that alone can heal, nourish, and transform it. The same sacred source that gave birth to each of us is needed to give meaning to our life, to nourish it with what is real, and to reveal to us the mystery, the divine purpose to being alive.

Because humanity has a central function in the whole of creation, what we deny to ourself we deny to all of life. In denying the feminine her sacred power and purpose we have impoverished life in ways we do not understand. We have denied life its sacred source of meaning and divine purpose, which was understood by the ancient priestesses. We may think that their fertility rites and other ceremonies belonged only to the need for procreation or a successful harvest. In our contemporary culture we cannot understand how a deeper mystery was enacted, one that consciously connected life to its source in the inner worlds, a source that held the wholeness of life as an embodiment of the divine, allowing the wonder of the divine to be present in every moment.

The days of the priestesses, their temples and ceremonies are over, and because the wisdom of the feminine was not written down but transmitted orally (*logos* is a masculine principle), this sacred knowledge is lost. We cannot reclaim the past, but we can witness a world without her presence, a world which we exploit for greed and power, which we rape and pollute without real concern. And then we can begin the work of welcoming her back, of reconnecting with the divine that is at the core of creation, and learning once again how to work with the sacred principles of life. Without the intercession of the divine feminine we will remain in this physical and spiritual wasteland we have created, passing on to our children a diseased and desecrated world.

The choice is simple. Can we remember the wholeness that is within us, the wholeness that unites spirit and matter? Or will we continue walking down this road that has abandoned the divine feminine, that has cut women off from their sacred power and knowledge? If we choose the former we can begin to reclaim the world, not with masculine plans, but with the wisdom of the feminine, the wisdom that belongs to life itself. If we choose the latter we may attempt some surface solutions with new technology. We may combat global warming and pollution with scientific plans. But there will be no real change. A world that is not connected to its soul cannot heal. Without the participation of the divine feminine nothing new can be born.

RECLAIMING HER SACRED WISDOM

If the knowledge of the sacred feminine has been lost, how can we know what to do? Part of the wisdom of the feminine is to wait, to listen, to be receptive. A woman does not consciously know how to bring the light of a soul into her womb and help it to form a body. And yet this mystery takes place within her. Nor does she consciously know how to nourish this light with her own light, in the same way that she gives her blood to help the body to grow. She is the mystery of light being born into matter, and her pregnancy is a time of receptivity, waiting, listening and feeling what is happening within her. She and the Great Mother are one being, and if she listens within she is given the knowledge she needs.

We may have forsaken this simple feminine wisdom of listening, and in this information age awash with so many words it is easy to undervalue an instinctual knowledge that comes from within. But the sacred principles of life have never been written down: they belong to the heartbeat, to the rhythm of the breath and the flow of blood. They are alive like the rain and the rivers, the waxing and waning of the moon. If we learn to listen we will discover that life, the Great Mother, is speaking to us, telling us what we need to know. We are present at a time when the world is dying and waiting to be reborn, and all the words in our libraries and on the Internet will not tell us what to do. But the sacred feminine can share with us her secrets, tell us how to be, how to midwife her rebirth. And because we are her children she can speak to each of us, if we have the humility to listen.

How can we listen to what we do not know? How can we reclaim what we have lost so long ago? Every moment is new. The present moment is not just a progression of past moments, but is alive in its own way, complete and perfect. And it is the moment that demands our attention. Only in the moment can we be fully awake and respond to the real need. Only in the present moment can we be fully attentive. Only in the present moment can the divine come into existence. Men may make plans, but a mother attentive to her children knows the real need of the moment. She feels in her being the interconnectedness of all of life in a way that is veiled from the masculine. She knows one cannot make plans when there are so many variables, but one can respond with the wisdom that includes the whole and all of its connections. The divine feminine is asking us to be present in life in all of its wholeness, without judgment or plans. Then she can speak to us, reveal the mystery of her rebirth.

And because this is a birth, the feminine has to be present, not just as an idea but as a living presence within us, within both men and women; because although woman most fully embodies the divine feminine, part of her secret is also shared with men, just as a son carries part of his mother in a way hidden from her daughters. Yet to live the feminine is something we have almost forgotten: our patriarchal culture has denied her power and real wisdom, has sanitized her as much as it has divorced her from her magic that belongs to the rhythms of creation. But we need her, more than we dare realize.

However, to fully encounter the divine feminine, the creative principle of life, we must be prepared for her anger, for the pain that has come from her abuse. For centuries our masculine culture has repressed her natural power, has burnt her temples, killed her priestesses. Through his drive for mastery, and his fear of the feminine, of what he cannot understand or control, the patriarchy has not just neglected her, but deliberately tortured and destroyed. He has not just raped her, but torn the very fabric of life, the primal wholeness of which she is always the guardian. And the feminine is angry, even if her anger has been repressed along with her magic.

To welcome the feminine is to acknowledge and accept her pain and anger, and the part we have played in this desecration. Women too have often colluded with the masculine, denied their own power and natural magic, and instead accepted masculine values and ways of thinking. They have betrayed their own deepest self. But we must also be careful not to become caught in this darkness, in the dynamics of abuse, the anger and betrayal.

It is especially easy for women to become identified with the suffering of the feminine, her treatment by the masculine, to project their own pain and anger onto men. Then we are caught even more securely in this web that denies us any transformation. If we identify with the pain of the feminine we easily become an agent of her anger, rather than going deeper into the mystery of suffering, into the light that is always hidden in the darkness. Because in the depths of the feminine there is a deep knowledge that the abuse is also part of the cycle of creation. The Great Mother embodies a wholeness that contains even the denial of Herself, and we need Her wholeness if we are to survive and be reborn.

Real transformation, like any birth, needs the darkness as much as the light. We know that the feminine has been abused, just as the planet continues to be polluted. But the woman who has experienced the pain of childbirth, who knows the blood that belongs to birth, is always initiated in the darkness; she knows the cycles of creation in ways that are hidden to the masculine. She needs to give herself and her knowing to this present cycle of death and rebirth, and in so doing honor the pain she has suffered. Then she will discover that her magic and power are also being reborn in a new way, are being returned to her in ways that can no longer be contaminated by the masculine and its power drive. But without her full participation there is the danger of a stillbirth; then this present cycle of creation will not realize its potential.

First we need to acknowledge the suffering of the feminine, of the earth itself, or the light within the feminine will be hidden from us. We have to pay the price of our desires to dominate nature, of our acts of hubris. We are not separate from life, from the winds and the weather. We are a part of creation and we have to ask her forgiveness, to take responsibility for our attitude and actions. We need to go consciously into the next era, recognizing our mistakes. Only then can we fully honor and hear her. But there is always the possibility that we will

not take this step. That like defiant children we will not acknowledge the pain we have done to our mother, and will not
reclaim the wholeness that she embodies. Then we will remain
within the darkness that is beginning to devour our souls: the
empty promises of materialism, the fractured world of fanati-
cism. To take a step into maturity is always to acknowledge our
mistakes, the wrongs we have done.

GIVING BIRTH TO OUR OWN WHOLENESS

It is a real challenge to step into this matrix of the feminine, to
honor something so sacred and simple as the real wisdom of
life. But as we stand at the edge of our present global abyss we
need this wisdom more than we realize. How many times has
this world been brought to the edge of extinction, how many
times in its millions of years has it faced disaster? Now we have
created our own disaster with our ignorance and greed, and
the first step is to ask for the help of our mother and to listen
to her wisdom. Then we will find ourself in a very different
environment from the one we presently imagine. We will
discover that there are changes happening in the depths of
creation of which we are a part, and that the pollution and
pain we have caused are part of a cycle of life that involves
its own apparent destruction. We are not isolated, even in
our mistakes. We are part of the whole of creation even as we
have denied the whole. In our hubris we have separated ourself from life, and yet we can never be separate. That is just
an illusion of masculine thinking. There is no such thing as
separation. It is just a myth created by the ego.

Everything is part of the whole, even in its mistakes and
disasters. Once we return to this simple awareness we will

discover that there are changes taking place that demand our participation, that need us to be present. We will see that the axis of creation is shifting and something is coming alive in a new way. We are being reborn, not in any separate sense but as a complete whole. We do not have images in our masculine consciousness to think what this could be like, but this does not mean it is not happening. Something within us knows that the present era is over, that our time of separation is coming to an end. At present we sense it most apparently in the negative, knowing that the images of life no longer sustain us, that consumerism is killing our soul as well as the planet. And yet there is also something just beyond the horizon, like a dawn that we can sense even if we cannot see.

And this dawn carries a light, and this light is calling to us, calling to our souls if not yet to our minds. And it is asking for us to welcome it, to bring it into being. And if we dare to do this, to say "yes" to this dawn, we will discover that this light is within us, and that something within each of us is being brought into being. We are part of a shared mystery: we are the light hidden within matter that is being awakened.

For too many centuries we have been caught in the myth of separation, until we have become isolated from each other and from the energies of creation that sustain us. But now there is a growing light that carries the knowing of oneness, the oneness that is alive with the imprint of the divine. This is what is being given back to us. This is the light that is awakening. The light of oneness is a reflection of the divine oneness of life, and we are each a direct expression of this oneness. And this oneness is not a metaphysical idea but something so simple and ordinary. It is in every breath, in the wing-beat of every butterfly, in every piece of garbage left on city streets. This oneness is life, life no longer experienced solely through the fragmented vision of the ego, but known within the heart, felt in the soul. This oneness is the heartbeat of life. It is creation's recognition of its Creator. In this oneness life celebrates itself and its divine origin.

The feminine knows this oneness. She feels it in her body, in her instinctual wisdom. She knows its interconnectedness just as she knows how to nourish her own children. And yet until now this knowing has not carried the bright light of masculine consciousness. It has remained hidden within her, in the darkness of her instinctual self. And part of her pain has been that she has not known how to use her knowing in the rational and scientific world we inhabit. Instead of valuing her own knowledge she has played the games of the masculine, imitating his thinking, putting aside her knowledge of relationships and her sense of the patterns that belong to creation.[2]

Now it is time for this wisdom of the feminine to be combined with masculine consciousness, so that a new understanding of the wholeness of life can be used to help us to heal our world. Our present scientific solutions come from the masculine tools of analysis, the very mind-set of separation that has caused the problems. We cannot afford to isolate ourself from the whole anymore, and the fact that our problems are global illustrates this. Global warming is not just a scientific image or concept but a dramatic reality. Combining masculine and feminine wisdom we can come to understand the relationships between the parts and the whole, and if we listen we can hear life telling us how to redress this imbalance.

There is a light within life, known to the alchemists as the *lumen naturae*, that can speak to us, speak to the light of our own awareness. There is a primal dialogue of light to light, which is known to every healer as she listens to the body of her patient and allows it to communicate with her, allows its light to speak to the light within her. Through this dialogue of light she comes to know where to place her hands, the herbs that are needed, the pressure points to be touched. This direct communication is combined with the knowledge of healing she has learned, allowing an alchemy to take place that can re-awaken energy within the patient, realign the body and soul. This is how real healing happens, and what is true for the individual is also true for the world, except that we are both the patient and the healer. The world's wounds and imbalance are our wounds and imbalance, and we have within us the knowledge and understanding to realign ourselves and the world. This is part of the mystery of life's wholeness.

The feminine can give us an understanding of how all the diverse parts of life relate together, their patterns of relationship, the interconnections that nourish life. She can help us to see consciously what she knows instinctively, that all is part of a living, organic whole, in which all the parts of creation communicate together, and that each cell of creation expresses the whole in a unique way. An understanding of the organic wholeness of life belongs to the instinctual knowing of the feminine, but combined with masculine consciousness this can be communicated in words, not just feelings. We can combine the science of the mind and the senses with inner knowing. We can be given a blueprint of the planet that will enable us to live in creative harmony with all of life.

A NEW MAGIC IS PRESENT

What does it mean to reclaim the feminine? It means to honor our sacred connection to life that is present in every moment. It means to realize that life is one whole and begin to recognize the interconnections that form the web of life. It means to realize that everything, every act, even every thought, affects the whole. And it also means to allow life to speak to us. We are constantly bombarded by so many impressions, by so much media and advertising, that it is not easy to hear the simple voice of life itself. But it is present, even within the mirage of our fears and desires, our anxieties and expectations. And life is waiting for us to listen: it just needs us to be present and attentive. It is trying to communicate to us the secrets of creation so that we can participate in the wonder that is being born.

We have been exiled from our own home, sold a barren landscape full of soulless fantasies. It is time to return home, to claim what belongs to us, the sacred life of which we are a part. This is what is waiting for us, and its signs are appearing around us. They are not just in our discontent, in our sense that we have been exploited and lied to. They are in a quality of magic that is beginning to appear, like the wing-beats of angels we cannot see but can feel. We are being reminded of what we really are, of the divine presence that is within ourself and within life. We long for this magic, for a life that unites the inner and outer worlds. And this other is already with us in ways we would not expect. We just have to be open and receptive, to say "yes" to what we cannot see or touch, but can feel and respond to. And for each of us this meeting of the worlds will be different, unique, because we are each different, unique. It is the sacred within life speaking to us in our own language. Maybe for the gardener it speaks in the magic of plants, for the mother in something unexpected in the ways of her children—always it is something glimpsed but not yet known—a promise we know we have been waiting for. Children themselves feel it first, but for them it is not so unusual; it is part of the air they breathe, the light they live in. They have not yet been completely banished, and maybe they will grow into a world in which this magic remains.

The mystery of the divine feminine speaks to us from within her creation. She is not a distant god in heaven, but a presence that is here with us, needing our response. She is the divine returning to claim her creation, the real wonder of what it means to be alive. We have forgotten her, just as we have forgotten so much of what is sacred, and yet she is always part of us. But now she needs to be known again, not just as a myth, as a spiritual image, but as something that belongs to the blood and the breath. She can awaken us to an expectancy in the air, to an ancient memory coming alive in a new way. She can help us to give birth to the divine that is within us, to the oneness that is all around us. She can help us to remember our real nature.

The soul of the world is crying to be heard,
and only those who have suffered can fully recognize it.
If women can come to know the sacred dimension of their
own and the earth's suffering, if they can see that it is
part of the mysterious destiny of the soul of our
world, if they can look beyond their own
personal pain and anger to accept
their larger destiny, then the
forces of life can flow in
a new way.

2

The Contribution of the Feminine

Life is an interconnected whole, and the energy of life flows through the web of connections that link part to part. Human beings can work with this energy, to help it flow freely on all levels and to reach every part of the whole. Now, at this time of transition as we move out of one stage in our evolution and into the next, we are being asked to do this—to work consciously with the energy that flows through the web of connections—so that the oneness of life can shape the consciousness of the next age.

The knowledge we need for this work lies in the wisdom of the feminine. As a part of the sacred mystery of creation, the feminine is always attuned to the oneness, the interconnected wholeness of life. While the bright light of masculine consciousness sees each object standing out clear and distinct, the diffuse, more hidden consciousness of the feminine sees the patterns of the relationships that connect them. The feminine has an instinctive understanding of these connections—how they are made; how they can become damaged, torn, destroyed; how they can be repaired.

Every woman carries this wisdom within her. She feels the pulse of life, consciously or unconsciously, as intimately as she feels her own blood pulsing through her veins. Her knowing is not abstract, but lived in her very body in a way that is inaccessible to men. In the cells of her body she carries the light of the consciousness of oneness, a light that is not present in men's bodies.

This consciousness has long been held secret, driven underground through centuries of masculine rejection and abuse, hidden even from women's own conscious knowing. But women still carry it, and now the time has come for it to be made known. For if that light can be brought into consciousness, then it can travel through the web of connections, awakening centers of consciousness within all of humanity. Humanity will have access to the wisdom, power, and love that it needs to take the next step in its spiritual evolution: to learn to function in oneness, as a dynamic, interrelated whole. Without this awakening, patterns of energy-flow around the planet will remain dormant, or function on a lower level, and once again humanity will have missed an opportunity.

Women hold the key to this work: only they have access to the light of conscious oneness that lives in their bodies. There are reasons why they might hesitate to take it on. They carry in their ancient memories the scars of persecution and often a deep anger toward the masculine. They still fear the power of the patriarchy, its potential for abuse. And the danger is real. But those who look after the destiny of our planet have balanced the forces of light and dark so as to give humanity the optimum opportunity to make this step. Women now have the choice: to stay hidden, or to bring their inner knowing into the outer world.

The choice is a difficult one, because the knowledge held within the physical bodies of women is covered in the pain and anger that have resulted from centuries of abuse. To reach the wisdom of oneness that lies hidden beneath it will mean to face not only the threat of more abuse, but also the real pain of the past and the anger it has engendered. It will mean becoming vulnerable to a frightening degree. It is for each woman to make the choice for herself. This is the nature of free will. Yet the need is pressing. The physical body of the feminine is itself the connection between heaven and earth, the connection through which oneness is made manifest. Through it, the energy of oneness becomes a part of the earth, available to life. Without the full participation of the feminine, that energy remains unavailable, and the joy and sense of belonging to God that it carries cannot be lived. Only women can make this next step. After centuries of suffering, women now have the freedom to deny us all the future.

To take this step now demands that women face their suffering in the full light of consciousness. But women more than men know the sanctification that comes from suffering—not the self-inflicted or self-indulgent suffering that we hide behind as protection from life or ourselves, but the suffering that life brings us naturally as part of the destiny of the soul. Women know that kind of suffering in their own childbearing bodies; they know that it belongs to the mystery of life, to the mysteries of birth and rebirth. They know that, offered consciously back to the Creator, it can make life sacred. A woman knows in her body that through suffering the immortal spirit takes on form, the soul comes into manifestation, the divine enters life.

And since women carry within the cellular structure of their bodies the imprint of all creation, they carry the consciousness not only of their own suffering but also of the suffering of the earth: the wounds and desecration caused by a patriarchal culture that sees God only in heaven. The pain many women feel in the core of their being is also the unacknowledged pain of the earth cut off by this masculine way of thinking from the divine—exploited, damaged, and desecrated by our patriarchal culture. This suffering too needs to be accepted and sanctified, so that the energy of life can flow freely within the earth. The earth has cried and women have heard its cry, felt its tears.

Women can acknowledge the earth's deep sorrow and wounding, and through the heart offer it back to God who is the source of all sorrow and all joy. It has been said that God enters through a wound, and through the earth's sorrow a healing can take place; the consciousness of divine love can be infused into the hidden places of the earth as well as into the bodies of women. This love can link the two worlds in a way that has not happened before. Through that connection, activated in women's bodies through their sanctification of their own and the earth's suffering, grace can flow into the world. The meaning and magic that lie at the core of creation, the secret of the word *"Kun!"* ("Be!"),[1] can come alive.

The soul of the world is crying to be heard, and only those who have suffered can fully recognize it. If women can come to know the sacred dimension of their own and the earth's suffering, if they can see that it is part of the mysterious destiny of the soul of our world, if they can look beyond their own personal pain and anger to accept their larger destiny, then the forces of life can flow in a new way. The imprint of the divine face can become visible in this world and the glory of oneness be known, and once again life can become sacred.

And yet we wait, reluctant to take a step into the unknown. We look around for comfort and security, even spiritual security. The feminine knows that the darkness is real and life-giving. She also knows the secrets of love and longing, because love is a feminine mystery. Yet she is reluctant to live her real passion, bring it out into the light of consciousness, just as the masculine is reluctant to leave the safety of what he knows, the positions of power he has established over the centuries, and step into the fertile darkness of the unknown.

Each time when humanity has come to this step it has turned back. Can this moment be different? Can we walk forward together, men and women, naked, unafraid of either the light or the darkness?

In a dream, told by a woman, a window is open, and a dove is flying towards the window, carrying a letter at her feet. In fact she is flying upon this letter, the letter carrying her. It is written by two children of the Orient whose parents are separated, one living in the Orient, one in the Occident. The children want their parents to come together again. This letter has such a deep call, such longing in it.

This is our own call and longing, to heal the separations of feminine and masculine, of East and West, and beyond that, to make a new link between future and past, the unknown and the known, the divine and this world—to take this next step in our evolution.

It is time to leave the antagonism behind, as a ship leaves the shore behind. Only life and love can guide us—all our beliefs and convictions only constellate a more dangerous conflict. Certain new currents have come near the shore to take us on our journey, and we can let them take us. And there is an urgency to this voyage, although events will unfold in their own time.

To live this dream of reconnection takes courage and foolishness. We are uneasy, uncertain, as we should be at the beginning of such a venture. But only by living it completely, without excuses, can we claim what is waiting for us. The beyond is beckoning; it has sent its emissaries of both light and darkness. Nothing is certain, but there is a magic waiting to happen; many dreams now can become real.

What this will mean will be different for each of us, because taking this next step requires that we live our uniqueness. We are being asked to behave as adults, prepared to take our own destiny and the destiny of the world in both hands. Women, each one in her own way, are being asked to step into the light of a new consciousness, to acknowledge and make sacred their own and the earth's suffering, to make their deeper wisdom known. Men are being asked to give up their hierarchies of power and dominance and make room for the feminine wisdom of connectedness as it can manifest in their own lives. Then the light of conscious oneness can infuse the whole web of connected life and new centers of consciousness can be opened. Then a new link of love will be forged through the hearts of the whole of humanity, the heart of the world will open, the two worlds come together—and the future will be born.

But the future has already been born. We are the link of love; we are the heart of the world; we are the future. Yet we don't see it. And we will not see it until we can step out of the shadows of the past. It will mean leaving behind all we consider precious, letting go of all our attachments to what is ending. And that will not be easy. In times of transition the illusions of the last age close fiercely around us; our attachments cling to us, more tightly that ever. The illusions of a dying age are very dangerous, because they carry the potency of all our unlived dreams, of everything that was never fulfilled. Are we prepared to give up everything we wanted for ourselves? Are we prepared to step into the unknown, empty of all attachment, expecting nothing? For this is the only way to take the step we are being asked to take, to live the oneness of divine love in this world.

There are also forces that stand in the way of this new awakening, that want to keep us in the grip of their power structures, to keep us enslaved with greed and self-centered desires. They have even polluted the spiritual arena, where self-improvement rather than selfless service is encouraged. One cannot sell devotion or market how to give oneself. Love has no power structures or hierarchies; it is not for sale. It passes freely from heart to heart along the web of oneness that connects us all. But in the dense patterns of our worldly thought-forms we have forgotten that the real gifts of God, like the sunlight, are always free. For centuries the secrets of divine love and the knowledge of oneness have passed freely from heart to heart in secret, while the world went about its unheeding ways. But the need of the time is that it come out into the light now, so that it can be lived in the world.

A web of light has been created around the world to help us make this transition. Through this web the invisible is already becoming visible, the signs of God are already revealing themselves in a new way. In the energy of divine oneness the opposites have already come together. But love needs us to bring this potential into manifestation, to make it part of the fabric of daily life. Without our participation the potential will ebb into a fading promise of something that might have happened.

This is the work of lovers, of those in service to His love. Lovers know how to give themselves to the moment, to be awake in the eternal now. They are not afraid of the consequences of their actions because they know that only divine love is real. They honor their soul's pledge to witness the Beloved's[2] one-ness. In the mirror of their heart a secret is being born, and in the network of lovers this secret is coming alive. Humanity has forgotten that the world can only be transformed through love, that love is the greatest power in creation. But God's lovers have always known this, and long ago they gave themselves to the work of divine love.

Without this central note of pure love, the future will remain just a dream and the patterns of the past will close more tightly around us. With love, joy will return, and joy will cleanse away the pollution of the world, the negative thought-forms and patterns of greed that devour so much of our energy and life force. When joy returns to the hearts and lives of humanity, the whole world will come alive in a new way. The soul of the world will sing the oneness of God and we will know why we are here.

*Banishing God to the heavens, we lost touch with the
sacredness of the earth and its many forms of life. We are
slowly becoming conscious of this imbalance and the danger
caused by the rejection of the Goddess. We see how our whole
planet is suffering from the abuses of masculine technology. At
the same time, many patterns of the repression of the feminine
have surfaced. Women have had to confront both individual
and collective experiences of abuse. The masculine power
principle has been recognized as responsible for tremendous
feminine suffering, to the individual and to the ecosystem.
In response to this deep and dangerous imbalance,
the feminine aspect of the divinity, the Goddess,
has begun to be reinstated. Reinstating the
Goddess means restoring the sacredness
of a nurturing, all-embracing divinity.
God's masculine omnipotence and
transcendence need to be
balanced by the feminine
aspects of care and
nearness.*

3

Patriarchal Deities
and the Repression of the Feminine

In our Western Judeo-Christian culture we have been dominated by a masculine, heavenly God. In the Judaic tradition there is an avenging God who banished us from paradise. The God of wrath of the Old Testament was replaced by a Christian God of kindness and love. In the figure of Christ, the Christian God was incarnated, but then ascended from the cross back to his heavenly Father. Furthermore, the Old Testament God of wrath remained in the Christian tradition in sermons of hell-fire and the emphasis on human failings and sinfulness. Over the last centuries Puritan and Victorian morality engraved fear rather than love into our religious culture, stressing human inadequacy and leaving a trail of repression and neurosis. How much has this image of a remote and wrathful deity influenced our relationship to the divine?

The masculine divinity belongs to the heavens. Under the dominance of a masculine god, we have developed science and the ability to control aspects of our environment. But we have become separate from the sacred interdependence of creation and no longer live in a daily relationship with the divinity of all forms. Once when my teacher was giving a lecture, she used the term "God's feet." A member of the audience asked, "How can the Absolute have feet?" She responded, "How many feet has a spider, how many feet has a horse?" If God is totally elevated to the heavens it is easy to lose touch with the divine in everyday life. We come to know Him only as a distant authoritarian father. Our present culture resonates with the feelings of alienation and individual impotence that reflect the remoteness of our masculine God. We easily feel uncared-for and unprotected, isolated, no longer an integral part of the great wholeness of life.

The sacred wholeness of life belongs to the feminine aspect of the divine, the Great Goddess. For Her every act is sacred; every blade of grass, every creature is a part of the Great Oneness. In contrast to His awe-inspiring transcendence, She embodies the caring divine presence. The Native Americans, among other tribal cultures, honored this aspect of the Great Mother:

> The Great Spirit is our father, but the Earth is our mother. She nourishes us; that which we put into the ground she returns to us, and healing plants she gives us likewise.[1]

Like the Native American, the mystic is familiar with the caring, all-embracing aspect of the divine. Experiences of oneness, which are so central to the mystical path, include every atom of creation; every leaf of every tree is experienced as sacred.[2] One of the first mystical experiences is often a sense of divine presence, and the knowledge of the Beloved's tenderness and closeness grows with our devotion and practices. Like Zulaikha in her love for Joseph,[3] we seek and find our Beloved's name in everything. The practice of the presence of God is essential work for the wayfarer, who shares every activity with her Beloved. Cooking, we stir the pot with Him; walking, we feel Him accompanying us. In difficulty we talk to Him, in delight we praise Him. Repeating the *dhikr* or *mantra* we constantly remember the Beloved's name with love. We bring Him whom we love into every corner of our life.

In our meditation and our daily life we come to know what our culture has forgotten. We hear the sacred song of divine presence in the marketplace and in our hearts. But we also feel the sorrow of a society that is dominated by a collective sense of divine absence.

Banishing God to the heavens, we lost touch with the sacredness of the earth and its many forms of life. We are slowly becoming conscious of this imbalance and the danger caused by the rejection of the Goddess. We see how our whole planet is suffering from the abuses of masculine technology. At the same time, many patterns of the repression of the feminine have surfaced. Women have had to confront both individual and collective experiences of abuse. The masculine power principle has been recognized as responsible for tremendous feminine suffering, to the individual and to the ecosystem. In response to this deep and dangerous imbalance, the feminine aspect of the divinity, the Goddess, has begun to be reinstated. Reinstating the Goddess means restoring the sacredness of a nurturing, all-embracing divinity. God's masculine omnipotence and transcendence need to be balanced by the feminine aspects of care and nearness.

But we are wrong to restrict our image of a transcendent deity to the patriarchal power-drive. Reinstating the feminine, all-embracing Goddess should not mean denying our instinctual awe for His omnipotence. Nor should the feminine's fear of repression and abuse result in rejecting His majesty. Intimacy and awe are two aspects of God's oneness. The divine is both far and near, as expressed in the *hadîth qudsî,* "My heaven and My earth contain Me not, but the heart of My devoted servant contains Me."

... women have inherited as a result of patriarchal culture this masculine mind that dismisses their own feminine understanding, which then produces all these negative thoughts and arguments that undermine their own instinctual knowledge. And I don't think it was meant to be like that. I think there must be some way to develop a feminine mind that is in harmony with feminine consciousness, which would then work very beautifully and help us to understand all the patterns of relationship within life and how life works.

4

Feminine Consciousness
and the Masculine Mind

*Transcript of a talk given September, 2006
in Hittfeld, Germany[1]*

*This is a response to a question from a woman
in the audience to do with doubts.*

In response to your question, I'd like to share with you a by-product of my recent investigation into the subject of darkness[2] that primarily concerns women. In my work I have often wondered why so many women seem to be caught in so much mental negativity, and also so much *emotional* negativity. Because in my memories of previous lives, women who lived a spiritual life weren't like that. They were attuned to the magic of creation; they understood and were in service to the secrets of life and the ways the outer world could be nourished by the inner world. They lived in harmony with the world, with life. I don't think they knew what a doubt was. I don't think lack of self-esteem entered their horizon. And so, for the last twenty years, I've been trying to put this inner image I have of the feminine onto the women involved in spiritual life whom I have encountered, and it doesn't seem to fit. So I've wondered what has happened. And I've come to understand that it has to do partly with the mind.

The mind is a very beautiful thing; it can do all sorts of extraordinary things. Yes, it can think ridiculous thoughts on its own, but its nature is not negative. And yet, I see how it can affect women and appear to undermine them so much of the time, without them knowing it. It doesn't honor what is sacred within them or help them to live it. And it creates doubts that undermine their natural integrity. It often seems to poison them more than it helps them. I don't think the mind is meant to do this. I think the mind is really meant to be a helpful tool for living in this world. When you don't need to be in this world and go deep in meditation, you leave it behind. You become empty of thoughts and can become immersed in a deep stillness. But in waking consciousness it is a very necessary and useful tool, and it is really something very, very beautiful.

Now, what I have come to understand is that men, for centuries, have developed the thinking capacity of the mind. And, being men, they have developed a masculine mind. Until recently, girls didn't even have the opportunity to go to school. In fact, there are parts of the world where girls *still* don't go to school. And so the feminine education of the mind never happened in our culture. All our education is geared for the masculine mind, and the masculine mind is quite different from the feminine mind.

For example, the masculine mind thinks linearly. It's goal oriented—there's a problem, we figure out how to solve it. Masculine consciousness is quite focused. The feminine consciousness, on the other hand, is relational. It looks around and it asks, is nature focused? Is a squirrel, say, completely focused on being a squirrel? No. The squirrel makes a relationship to everything around it and in the midst of all those patterns of relationship it knows where the nut is, and it knows how to leap from branch to branch to get the nut. And feminine consciousness, by its very nature, works in the same way; it feels all these different patterns of relationship and how they work together. It is not linear; it functions quite, quite differently. It has a different purpose. For example, when a woman has four children to look after and is cooking at the same time, she cannot just be focused on *one* thing.

So women's consciousness can hold many things in relationship all the time. But what happened in the last centuries is that as women became educated in schools and colleges designed by men to teach men how to think in a masculine way, they absorbed this masculine consciousness. They overlaid their feminine relational understanding with a masculine mind. And because they wanted to succeed in a man's world, they focused their energy on this masculine way of thinking. But it doesn't fully work for them—it is not in harmony with their real nature, and instead can create a deep anxiety in the feminine consciousness that something is wrong, but they don't know what it is. And so, somehow, this masculine consciousness in the woman then turns back upon itself and instead of being a tool to function in the world it also becomes a means by which women undermine themselves. And this masculine mind has, of course, for centuries been trained how to undermine women. Men have used their masculine mind to dismiss women's power and natural way of being very effectively for centuries. They know all the arguments to dismiss these "crazy, irrational" women.

So, possibly when this masculine mind encounters this feminine consciousness it just attacks it. And then the women believe it—women must live in torment when this happens. Women have inherited this masculine mind that dismisses their own feminine understanding, which then produces all these negative thoughts and arguments that undermine their own instinctual knowledge. And I don't think it was meant to be like that. I think there must be some way to develop a feminine mind that is in harmony with feminine consciousness, which would then work very beautifully and help us to understand all the patterns of relationship within life and how life works. Because most men in the West appear to have *no* natural understanding of how life works. They can understand how *machines* work more easily than how life functions.

So anyway, that's just a suggestion for women who have these minds that create doubts. If you don't have one of those minds then you are very fortunate.

And to go along with that, this recent exploration of darkness also showed me—and again this mainly applies to women— how through the cracks in their own psychological make-up a certain negative energy comes in that makes women suffer more than they need to. And I don't think this negative energy actually belongs to the individual woman. I think it has much more to do with the suffering of the earth, with the abuse that has been inflicted on what is natural within life. Just as there is physical pollution so there's a kind of psychic pollution in the world. It's as if the natural flow of life no longer takes place; it no longer flows from the inner to the outer and from the outer to the inner.

So it's rather like one of those backwaters in a river that seem to just go around and around and attract all sorts of pollution. The water no longer flows cleanly; it no longer sparkles. And that is the psychic soup in which we live. Nothing gets purified. And I think women, because they are closer to life and closer to the flow of life, take it in more than men. Men live in it but they're focused and they're just not open to it in the same way. And so I think it creates a lot of problems for women. And of course, the more open and the more sensitive and the more evolved you are, and the more aware of your instinctual nature and open to the earth, the more you get affected by this negativity, even attacked, and you don't even know what's happening.

And then, just to add a little something to this, if you're a really sincere woman you work on your problems. And you try to resolve them. And what you don't realize is, it's not always your problem. And you can work on it *forever*. All it takes is a little wound inside of you—maybe you feel sorry for yourself, maybe you feel left out, maybe you have a tendency to be jealous. We all have those little character quirks. But you can get caught in it endlessly because through your wound comes the energy, the pain which does not belong just to you, but to the greater wound. Through your own wound comes this primal soup. So what might be a little jealousy becomes an all-engulfing jealousy. And then you suffer and you go on suffering and the harder you work on it the more you suffer. And when you've cleaned out that little problem you find there's another problem and it comes in again, and so it goes on.

I used to always think women had the best of it because unlike men they have this direct access to the energy of life and the beauty of creation. And although like everyone they have problems and difficulties that need to be worked on, they always have life's essential purity within them. As my Sheikh Bhai Sahib said, women are always pure.[3] They already have all the higher energies in their *chakras*. They don't have to work and purify themselves in the same way that men do, which is why traditionally men often needed ascetic practices on the spiritual path. But nowadays I am not so sure that it is easy to be a woman.

Anyway, I don't know if you find that helpful, but I just wanted to pass it along as it kind of came my way.

There are many different qualities of feminine wisdom,
from the understanding of the healing power of herbs to the
deep, lived knowledge of the feminine nature of the soul's
relationship with God, the soul's true state of receptivity to
the divine. So many of these qualities have been lost; so many
priestesses have been killed, wise women burned. And
yet the real wisdom remains, because it belongs to life
itself. In the cells and in the soul of every woman
this ancient knowing is waiting to be awakened,
so that once again the sacred feminine can make
her contribution, can help the world
come alive with love
and joy.

5

The Sacred Feminine
and Global Transformation

May we be those
who shall renew this existence.
ZARATHUSTRA

The feminine holds the mystery of creation. This simple and primordial truth is often overlooked, but at this time of global crisis, which also carries the seeds of a global transformation, we need to reawaken to the spiritual power and potential of the feminine. Without the feminine nothing new can be born, nothing new can come into existence—we will remain caught in the materialistic images of life that are polluting our planet and desecrating our souls.

We see around us a world being destroyed by greed and consumerism, and feel within us the hunger of our soul for a way of life that acknowledges the sacred within all of life. And deeper, there is the cry of the soul of the world, the primal cry that comes from the depths of creation when the divine light that belongs to life is being lost. At this time we need to reclaim what has been denied, what has been abandoned in the pursuit of our materialistic dreams. We need to return to the core of our being, to where the sacred comes into existence. And the mystical feminine holds the key to this work of redemption and transformation.

The patriarchal era has denied women access to their real power. The patriarchy systematically repressed the power of the Goddess and the mystical teachings of the feminine. And yet this wisdom is still present, just as is the deep knowing every woman has of the interconnectedness of all of life. And every woman carries in her spiritual centers the sacred light of creation. Without this light she could not conceive and give birth, she could not participate in the greatest mystery of bringing a soul into life: giving the spiritual light of a soul a physical form out of the substance of her own body. Men do not have this sacred light within them in the same way; they have to purify and transform themselves to gain access to it. For a woman it is always present.

But women have to recognize their true spiritual nature and the transformative potential they carry within them, so that they can offer it back to life—for without its light the world will slowly die. The world needs the presence of women who are awake to their spiritual light, and who can work with the substance of life in order to heal and transform it.

The last era has created a separation between matter and spirit, and so matter has forgotten its sacred nature, its ability to transform. Life itself has become caught in the abusive thought-forms of the masculine that seek to dominate through power. Life needs to be freed of these constrictions, and matter itself needs to be reconnected to its spiritual potential. This is a work that belongs to women, to those who know the sacred nature of life and how to bring light into matter, just as they instinctively know how to bring a soul into this physical world. For a woman the physical and spiritual worlds can never be separate: she carries the light of the world within the cells of her body; her sexuality is a sacred offering to the Goddess. But she needs to consciously recognize this divine potential and deep knowing, so that she can live it in service to life and the need of the time.

For many centuries this spiritual knowing has been kept as a secret, hidden in order to protect it from the soldiers of the patriarchy and a church that repressed and persecuted the sacred feminine. Now many women are awakening to their natural spirituality, to their birthright, and also to the ancient tradition of feminine wisdom. They are seeking to reconnect to the sacred feminine in different ways—through creativity, healing, personal transformation, and other ways of empowerment.

QUALITIES OF FEMININE WISDOM

There are many different qualities of feminine wisdom, from the understanding of the healing power of herbs to the deep, lived knowledge of the feminine nature of the soul's relationship with God, the soul's true state of receptivity to the divine.[1] So many of these qualities have been lost; so many priestesses have been killed, wise women burned. And yet the real wisdom remains, because it belongs to life itself. In the cells and in the soul of every woman this ancient knowing is waiting to be awakened, so that once again the sacred feminine can make her contribution, can help the world come alive with love and joy.

Women know the wisdom of receptivity, of holding a sacred space. They can experience this in their bodies through the wonder of pregnancy; but the sacred feminine also knows how this works within the soul, how within the heart love and longing create a space for the divine to be born. Rûmî describes this eternal mystery of longing:

> Sorrow for His sake is a treasure in my heart.
> My heart is light upon light, a beautiful Mary with Jesus in the womb.

The feminine mysteries of love—the sanctity of longing, the receptivity of the heart that is always awake, waiting for her Beloved, for that moment when love comes secretly and sweetly—need to be reclaimed and honored. Only through receptivity can we give birth to the divine as a living presence within ourselves and within our life.

Women also know the importance of being rather than doing. We are addicted to activity, and have lost access to the primal power that comes from the still center of ourself. We think that the problems of the world and of ourselves can only be solved through "doing," not realizing that it is this focus on ceaseless activity that has created much of our present imbalance. Rather than always asking, "What should I do?," we can learn to reflect, "How should I be?" From this quality of being we listen, are attentive and aware. Through this simple but essential attitude, balance can return and a natural healing take place.

Just as a mother instinctively knows how to listen to her children so that she can respond to their real needs, so does the sacred feminine know how to listen inwardly and outwardly to life, to experience and participate in this sacred mystery of which we are a part. Then we can make a real relationship to life and to our soul, learn to live the life of the soul rather than the illusory life of the ego.

An understanding of relationships belongs to the feminine. Feminine wisdom understands the way connections between people, and the interconnectivity of life itself, hold something essential. Without these connections life cannot sustain itself. The sense of separation and isolation that our masculine culture has created is damaging and deeply painful. Because women are closer to creation than men are, they are more awake to the sorrow of the earth and can hear more clearly its cry of despair as our present culture continues to desecrate and pollute it. They know that this cannot continue much longer, that the light that belongs to life's sacred nature is being lost and that without this light nothing new can be born, there can be no transformation of life or human consciousness.

The innate wisdom of the feminine is needed to repair the damage we have done and to reconnect with what is sacred and essential within ourselves and within life. We need to understand our part within the sacred web of life, and how to relate once again to this primal wholeness that is a direct expression of the oneness of the divine.

It may be painful to be fully present, to hold this sacred connection with life, the earth, and our own soul. But without the presence of the sacred feminine and those who honor it within themselves, an essential substance will be lost to life. The spark of the divine that connects the creation to the Creator—the spark that holds the mystery of creation and the divine purpose of everything, every butterfly, every stone, the laughter of every child, and every lover's tear—will begin to dim.

SYMBOLIC CONSCIOUSNESS

Listening is an essential quality of receptivity. We need to learn to listen, to be inwardly and outwardly attentive, watching the signs that tell the real story of life. In our present masculine culture we are often too busy to listen to what life and the Beloved are trying to tell us. Instead we are caught in superficial experiences, and so we miss the meaning, the real purpose of our soul's life. Life is a direct expression of the divine, but unless we listen to this hidden presence, we experience only the distortions of our ego-self, its desires and anxieties. Life and the soul are always beckoning us, wanting to share the real wonder of being alive.

When we really listen we find ourselves present in another world full of meaning and magic. Then the signs within our outer life and in our dreams can speak to us, and take us on a journey far beyond the limited world of the ego. They open a door to the symbolic world that is just beneath the surface. It is from this inner dimension of images and symbols that the soul is nourished.[2] Recognizing and working with symbols requires an attitude of receptivity that allows the symbols to communicate in their own language. We come to know this ancient part of ourselves that is fully alive and knows the deeper destiny of our soul. And it is from this inner world that our everyday life too is nourished and we are given the direction we need.

When we work with the images of the inner world, a mysterious alchemy takes place as the conscious and unconscious come together, a *coniunctio* of opposites. The symbolic world opens us to a depth of meaning beyond our conscious self, to the archetypal world of the gods, where we can gain access to the way these powerful energies can work within our inner and outer lives. Then we begin the real work of the soul, a transformation that takes place in the very depths of our being that expands our consciousness and enriches our daily life with a deep sense of purpose. Each of us has our own journey to make, our own exploration of the inner world, and we are drawn into this dimension through different doorways: dreamwork, painting, music, sacred dance, or just sitting and being present with the images that arise from the depths. But each journey follows the timeless path of alchemical transformation, turning lead into gold, revealing the light that is hidden in the depths of our being.

This is an individual inner work, and yet it takes us beyond our individual self into the archetypal world where the symbols that belong to all of humanity also change and transform. Here we may discover that we are working not just with the substance of our own soul, but with the *anima mundi*, the soul of the world. The light we discover in our own depths is a spark of the World Soul, and the world needs this light to evolve. When we make this connection within our consciousness and within our imagination we begin to change the fabric of life.

Within the *anima mundi*, the primal forces of creation, the energies and powers that give form and meaning to all of life, are also being transformed. New symbols are arising from the depths to guide humanity on the next step of its evolution, for, in the words of Carl Jung, "The archetypal images decide the fate of man."[3]

Symbols act as a bridge between the inner and the outer worlds, allowing the energy and meaning of the inner to flow into the outer. They can bring into life primal energies that have not been polluted or conditioned, which we can then creatively channel. Through our conscious participation, our inner work and creative imagination, we can recognize and help bring into life these images that are needed to heal and transform our world. In previous eras this has been the work of the shaman, someone who was initiated and trained to work with the energies and images of the inner world. But at this time of global need this work is open to anyone whose attention is drawn inward, who is receptive and attentive to the images arising from the source of life.

Within each of us lies the knowledge of how the worlds work together, how the images of the soul come into being and determine the fate of humanity. This knowing is a part of life, part of the miracle of creation. And we may find that these new images are not the esoteric images that we have associated with the sacred, but are simple images that belong to life and to the patterns of interconnectivity and wholeness that are now making themselves known. For example, the Internet is a powerful, living image of life's interconnected oneness. As it becomes more and more present in our collective consciousness, it is more and more able to channel life's underlying energies in new ways. It is a power and life force of its own, able to evolve and adapt like a fast-changing organism, and, like other emerging images of our time, it is reconfiguring our consciousness, helping us to interact with life in new ways. And yet, like all symbols, it will only reveal its real potential when we relate to it with the correct attitude. If we see it just as a mechanical tool, its meaning and transformative potential will remain hidden.[4]

It can be a shock to think that the sacred is revealing itself in something as mundane as the technology of the Internet. But we need to be alert, to realize that the symbols that will shape the dream of the next era are likely to turn up in the places we least expect them—in ourselves, in the ordinariness of our daily lives. Then we can open ourselves to laughter and joy in the way the divine awakens us to a new way of being, turning our "spiritual" perception upside down once again!

Once we understand how these images arise from within life,[5] we will give them the correct attention, and start a creative dialogue with the symbolic world. This is part of the co-creative relationship that humanity is being offered, in which the individual can interact directly with the whole. As we help bring into being the symbols that can heal and nourish the soul of the world, we begin to live this responsibility. We take on our role as guardians of the planet, and we do so with the consciousness of oneness that includes and connects the sacred and the mundane, the inner and the outer, spirit and matter, the world's soul and body and our own, the individual and the planet.

THE NEED OF THE TIME

At this time of global crisis and imbalance women have a unique role. A woman feels the pulse of life as intimately as she feels her own blood pulsing through her veins. Her knowing is not abstract, but lived in her very body in a way that is inaccessible to men. In the cells of her body she carries the light of the consciousness of oneness, a light that is not present in men's bodies. In this light she knows the interconnectedness of life: how it is all a part of one living whole. This primal knowing needs to be given back to life, which is suffering under the masculine thought-forms of duality and separation. Our science has imposed upon life the image of the world as dead matter, something we can freely pollute and abuse. Feminine spiritual consciousness can reawaken the world to its sacred nature as a living being, and so help it to heal and transform. This simple acknowledgment of the divine within life is a powerful catalyst, transforming the life of the world just as a woman's awareness of the divine nature of the child growing within her can transform her own life.

To be aware of the divine within oneself and the divine within life and the world, and to know that it is all one, is a simple and powerful practice. It means to be present in life as it is—not as one would want it to be. And it means to live in the moment—there can be no transformation in the images of the past or the dreams of the future. Yet we are conditioned to look to the past and the future, rather than daring to live in the now. But only in the now can we participate in the creative mystery of life.

Alive in the present moment, one can see the significance of newly forming patterns of relationship and the way in which they belong to life's organic nature—an Indra's Net of dynamic possibilities. All around us there are signs of life recreating itself in new configurations as people begin to come together in new and different ways. The Internet and other tools of global communication are an essential part of this process, connecting people together regardless of the barriers of race, nationality, or physical location. Different people in all parts of the world are linking together, forming networks of shared interests—networks outside the control of any hierarchy or government, belonging to life itself.

And these patterns of connections are growing. But we have yet to fully understand that it is these patterns of relationship themselves that are so essential, that will provide the simple answers to the complexity of the times. Their deepest meaning and purpose lie not in the information they convey, but in the new, fluid, organic interrelationship of individuals and groups they are creating. Something is coming alive in a new way. While masculine analytic consciousness sees only the separate parts, feminine consciousness sees the whole pattern, and thus allows us to recognize what is really happening, to grasp the meaning of these fast-forming patterns and understand their sacred purpose within their seemingly mundane appearance, to know these signs as all a part of the organism of life recreating itself from the matrix of global oneness.

And through this awareness a spiritual energy can be given to these patterns of relationship, an energy that is needed for life to transform. On its own, life evolves slowly over millennia. But the light of consciousness dramatically speeds up this natural process, just as a catalyst accelerates the process of chemical transformation. Through the light of direct feminine knowing, life can quickly reconnect with its own divine nature, and the divine can transform life in ways that we cannot imagine. With our own ordinary consciousness we cannot heal and transform the world of the effects of our pollution—it would take too long to redeem what we have destroyed. But the presence of the divine can awaken the world to its magical and miraculous power. If we welcome the divine back into life, if we acknowledge her divine nature—then we can participate in life's re-creation, in the miracle that is waiting to happen.

Women know the suffering of the world and also the secrets of its transformation. They feel this suffering in the cells of their body. And in the cells of their body lie also the sacred light and instinctual wisdom that are needed to help the world to change and awaken. How each woman lives this knowing is unique to herself, but connections are being created now that are an organic part of life's regeneration. Some of these are connections between awakened individuals and groups through which the light of the sacred feminine can flow, communicating the primal mystery of how the divine can come alive within creation. The ancient mysteries of the feminine were never written down, but passed from woman to woman. As this wisdom resurfaces, once again women will create connections of light that honor what is sacred within themselves and within life. They will not deny the suffering of the world, but recognize it as a part of the process of transformation, the way "the divine enters through a wound."

Each age comes alive in its own way. We are entering an era of oneness in which we have to return to the sacred source of life that is within each of us.[6] We each have to recognize our own divinity and from this point of light make our unique contribution. And yet we are also one, part of an interrelated body of light we call the world. And in the core of creation a new light is being born, a light that carries the secrets of the future and of how the real miracle of life can once again be recognized and revered. This is the gift we are being given, the child of the future that is being born to each of us. And we are also the midwives of this destiny, this joy that is being returned to us, the primal joy of life celebrating its divine nature. Through the wisdom of the feminine we can all, each in our own way, give birth to this future.

*... women have this magical substance
in their being that has to do with the real mystery
of creation in which light takes on form and
takes on human consciousness and yet
remains true to its essential
nature.*

6

Women and
Healing the Earth

Transcript of a talk given October, 2007
in Auckland, New Zealand[1]

My Sheikh taught us, and this is generally not known in the West, that women have a certain spiritual substance in them that is not present in men. It has to do with the mystery of creation, with the fact that not only is a woman able to give birth physically but she is able to be a place where the light of the soul takes on human form and remains true to its essential nature. Now this is something really, really extraordinary.

It is a very beautiful thing, how that soul grows in the body and takes on shape. As this happens, the woman is overshadowed—every woman who is pregnant is overshadowed by the Great Mother. It's why, on one level, pregnant women have a special glow to them. I was able to see that with my daughter-in-law when she was pregnant with my two grandchildren. It's a very beautiful experience, and a very, very mysterious happening, and it is related to this certain substance in women that men do not have.

And now this substance needs to be given back to the earth, in order to revitalize the earth—because the earth has been horribly damaged and it has lost its ability to transmute spiritual light. Photosynthesis is a spiritual process as well as a physical one: like plants, human beings absorb spiritual light and it nourishes them, and the same is true for the earth. The earth actually absorbs spiritual light and transmutes it, and it grows as a spiritual being. This is part of all ancient rituals. But we no longer have those rituals, and now, because we have treated it so badly, we've actually damaged the light cells in the world.

You can do that to a human being. If human beings are treated really, really badly they regress inside and their spiritual potential becomes inaccessible to them. And that is why, on the spiritual path, human beings often have to be healed first before they can develop spiritually. I know that because that is what happened to me. When I came to my teacher I was very, very battered and I actually had to be put in a kind of incubator and healed first. Many of you who are involved with spiritual life and healing know that—if human beings are too damaged they can't realize their spiritual potential; first they have to be healed.

And the same is true of the world: the world has been terribly damaged and it needs to be healed. And women are needed in this healing, because women have this magical substance in their being that has to do with the real mystery of creation in which light takes on form and takes on human consciousness and yet remains true to its essential nature. At the moment of its birth, a child is complete. Later, when a child grows up, it can stop being true to its essential nature, but for that beautiful moment at birth it is complete. And it is this completeness that has to be given back to the earth.

Also, a certain redemption has to take place. One of the first steps in this is that women have to forgive the masculine, or men, for what they have done. There are a lot of women who are *not* prepared to do that and I don't blame them, because men have made a real mess. I mean, a real, *real* mess—people can see the ecological devastation but most people can't see the spiritual desecration that has been done. It is *horrible*. Certain temples in the inner worlds have been destroyed. You can't even go there anymore. So you have the McDonaldization of the outer world and now the inner world has been desecrated too.

Men can't heal the world. They don't know *how* to heal the world. It's women who have to do this healing. But first they have to learn to forgive the masculine for what it has done, because no healing can be done without forgiveness. If women put their anger into the spiritual body of the world—the anger they feel naturally toward everything that man has done—who knows what will happen. If the world were to get really, really angry—we can't even remember what a really angry active world is like (you actually may have some sense of it here in New Zealand because this is a volcanic country)—that is very dangerous. It would be cataclysmic. So first of all, there has to be forgiveness in order for the healing to happen.

And as far as I can see, this work has to be done by women. I find this very interesting because I have memories of past lives and not many women were involved in deep spiritual practice. In Buddhism, or even in Taoism, there were women, yes, but very few. In Sufism too. My Sheikh in India had a few women disciples, but mainly his disciples were men. Buddhism developed as a masculine, monastic practice mainly for men. At seven you were taken to the monastery and there weren't many women in the monastery. And all of the practices were designed by men, with men in mind. The really austere practices were designed to cut men off from their physical, instinctual self in order to give them access to higher states of consciousness.

Women should *never* do that. A woman should never cut herself off from her instinctual self, because a woman's instinctual self is sacred. It belongs to the sacred rhythm of life. It is very, very holy. But as I say, in the past era, spirituality was dominantly for men. And I have been very intrigued, being a spiritual teacher in the West, by the fact that seventy to eighty percent of people involved in spirituality in the West are *women. Why?* And also, I have known many old souls that weren't women before, who have come back now and reincarnated as women. *Why?* I have meditated on it a lot. Is it because men in our culture can't cope with devotional spirituality? That is too simplistic. From the other side, you see that a certain spiritual work needs to be done by women. That is one reason I can think of: at this time a certain spiritual work needs to be done that has to do with healing and transmuting the earth so it can once again function as a living spiritual organism, and that work can only be done by women.

Now how that happens is very mysterious. For women their instinctual self, their bodies, their sexuality, their physical cycles are sacred in a way that is not true for men. And that means that an energy, a higher energy, can come down through a woman's spiritual vehicles into her body, and through her body into the physical body of the world. This is as far as I can understand it: as it comes into the physical body of the world, it brings with it this sacred substance in a woman which is always completely pure. Our Sheikh said that a woman is always pure. A woman can never be impure. And he used an example that women are like gold—if you put gold in the latrine it still remains gold. A woman has to be pure, because every child that is born is pure. This is a sacred creative process, so that substance in a woman is always pure. In a man it isn't. In order to realize that purity as a man you have to do many, many austere practices—very, very disciplined, austere practices over many years, practices that are rarely done nowadays, mostly because people don't have time. But in women this substance is always pure. They are part of the sacred substance of life and they can bring this pure substance into the world if they allow it to happen. If they are angry, if they are resentful, if they have hostility, it can't get through; in fact it *mustn't* get through, because it could awaken the anger of the earth.

My sense is that in the next fifty years there will be circles of women all around the planet who will be trained to do this work, who will be spiritually activated. And once that pure energy goes into the world, then it can heal. First of all, this energy can heal the damage that has been done to the spiritual body of the world. And then the spiritual body of the world can be activated, and the world reenergized. This work can speed up a process that would otherwise take a very long time. Because the cycles of nature are much, much longer than human cycles. The cycles of nature normally take thousands of years, or hundreds of thousands of years. But a human being can be like an alchemical catalyst and speed up the process of change. If there were no human intervention, spiritually, the world would heal itself over thousands of years—thousands of years to heal the damage we have done to it in the past three to four hundred years.

Without this intervention the world would regress. The magic in the world, the wisdom and the light in the world would no longer be accessible to humanity, and we would enter a new dark age. It might just take the form of a materialistic civilization that goes on for a thousand years until everything in the world is depleted. Or the dark age might be a complete breakdown of civilization as happened in Europe after the fall of the Roman Empire. But through the spiritual work of women— and only *women* can do this work; a man can't, and he is also not allowed to because he has done so much damage—then what could take a thousand years can take twenty, thirty, or forty years.

Question from man in audience: What then is the role of men?

Llewellyn Vaughan-Lee: The role of men is to protect women in this work and to protect this work—to value it and to consciously protect it. This is the role of the masculine as the protector—that you honor this work that is being done by women and you don't allow it to be interfered with. How that will get played out I don't know. There are so many negative forces in the world that don't want this work to be done, that don't want the world to be activated again, and that oppose having the women regain their power because women's power is decentralized, it is organic, it cannot be manipulated, it cannot be controlled— it is life.

*The physical world needs to be realigned
with its own energy source, with the life force that
is within it. The quickest way to realign anything is to
acknowledge its divine nature. Through the interaction of
humanity and life, conscious awareness of God interacts with
the unconscious knowing of God that exists within all of
creation. Creation can then return to the divine axis
that is at its core, and through this axis life
will flow in its divine purity,
its essential joy.*

*Because our patriarchal culture has
separated the spiritual and the physical, one of
the first steps in healing the planet is to acknowledge
the spiritual potential of matter, to align the world with
its divine consciousness. Women can do this work more easily
than men can. It is a part of their instinctual spiritual
nature. This is one of the reasons that in the West more
women than men are attracted to spiritual life—
there is a work for which
they are needed.*

7

The Energy of Matter

If the eye of your heart is open
In each atom there will be
One hundred secrets.
ATTÂR [1]

WORKING WITH THE NAME OF GOD

In the center of the world an energy source exists that has not yet been accessible. As the world awakens,[2] this energy will gradually become available, and we will learn how to use it. This energy has to do with the fundamental structure of matter, but it is quite different from atomic energy. Atomic energy is released through splitting the atom, a process of division. It belongs to the end of the era of opposition, of life based upon dualism. The energy sources of the future reflect the dynamics of a new era, based upon synergy and the inherent oneness of life.

We have become used to the constrictions of matter, fought against its limitations, learnt how to fly and talk across the world. Now we can learn how matter is alive and can be awakened. The energy of matter is so great as to appear unlimited. We have glimpsed it through splitting the atom, the dynamics of separation. But the flow of relating, of coming together, can release another form of energy within matter. At its core this has to do with the union of spirit and matter. When human consciousness and the physical world work in harmony, a new era can begin.

Every atom in creation spins freely on its own axis of love. There is no constriction in this motion. The real constriction is the denial of our divinity and the divinity of matter. This denial is what silences the song of the world and closes the door to the light hidden in matter. As the world became identified as a place in which the divine is absent, a solely physical reality divorced from the spiritual realm, we veiled ourself from its magical nature. Influenced by both our attitude and our actions, the world began to die. Our environmental crisis is a direct result of our forgetfulness. It has taken many centuries for our inner attitude to create these physical conditions, but if one is to redeem a situation one needs to return to the core of the problem. Otherwise we are only treating the symptoms.

The physical world needs to be realigned with its own energy source, with the life force that is within it. The quickest way to realign anything is to acknowledge its divine nature. Through the interaction of humanity and life, conscious awareness of God interacts with the unconscious knowing of God that exists within all of creation. Creation can then return to the divine axis that is at its core, and through this axis life will flow in its divine purity, its essential joy. The highest principle can come alive again within creation, and this will release the energy that is hidden in matter. This energy is what is needed to heal and redeem the world.

How do we realign the world? Through the simple practice of prayer and devotion. Through our inner alignment, and through our remembrance of God's presence, light and love flow into the world, awakening matter at the level of its deepest structures. As matter becomes realigned to its divine nature, it begins to vibrate at a higher frequency. It begins to sing, and this song is one of the ways it will heal itself. Song has always been a magical way of healing, and the song of the world has tremendous power. The work of the mystic is to be present as this happens, to witness the awakening of the world. Through our presence we add the ingredient of consciousness, which in its deepest sense is the knowing of the Beloved's name.

Spiritual traditions have always recognized the importance of the word, the *logos*, through which the first principle, the principle of the divine, can interact through the planes of manifestation while staying true to its essential nature. Through repeating His name in a *dhikr* or *mantra*, we consciously bring an awareness of the divine into our life, into the world of creation. We help the world remember its own divinity.

The name of God held in the hearts and consciousness of the friends of God is one of the secrets of creation. Shamans and other adepts have always understood how the name holds the magical potential of that which is named. The name of God has been repeated in the hearts and minds of God's lovers for centuries. It is carried on every breath, with the flow of the blood and each beat of the heart. Repeating the name of God with the flow of the breath, we align His name directly with the energy of life as it comes into creation, with the physical outpouring of His love. We consciously give an awareness of the divine principle in life to life.

The name of God has a great power, and when it is said with love and devotion, that power is magnified. Just as the name of God can awaken the divine love within our heart, so can it awaken the divine love within the cells of creation. As the name of God can align us with our divine nature, it can also align the whole of the world with the Unnamable Essence Sufis call Allâh.

In our human relationships, when we say the name of our beloved there is a special sweetness in our voice. When we hold our beloved in our arms and whisper his or her name, there is a special magic to our loving. What is done with our human lover can be done with the heart of the world. We can remind the world that it is loved, that we are all a part of a continual moment of ecstasy, of His love being born into the world again and again.

Our spiritual texts, written during the last era, do not describe how the remembrance of God works within creation. Our spiritual focus has been on the immaterial world, the inner realm of the soul. Volumes have been written on how our inner alignment leads us on our own path back to the Source. But we have lost the wisdom of how the name of God influences the world around us.

Previous eras understood how the many gods were a part of life, and how saying their sacred names could make magic, help the rains to come and the crops to grow. The advent of monotheism replaced the many gods with one God, whose home was in a celestial realm. While religion banished its image of God to heaven, the mystic always experienced the divine presence within the manifest world, knowing how every atom praises Him. But the mystical science of how the name of God interacts with life at the level of its fundamental structures—the cells, molecules, and atoms of matter—was hidden. Some minor forms of magic still remained, in which names, symbols, and geometric patterns could influence life. But chanting and sacred songs were used to turn our attention upward towards heaven. The deeper mysteries of how the oneness of life responds to the name of God, and how the divine name can be used to help the evolution of the planet, remained inaccessible except to those masters who worked within the axis of creation.

THE UNVEILING OF SPIRITUAL KNOWLEDGE

We think of the name of God as aligning us with a God who is within or above us. But in the mystery of oneness there is not the duality of inner and outer, above and below. We are all part of God's interpenetrating presence, and through us the Beloved's world can be aligned to the divine essence. Through the divine name His qualities can come into the world more easily, His revelation can make itself known more fully.

This revelation is a continually evolving dynamic process in which we are able to participate more and more consciously. Working with divine energy within creation is one of the ways in which we can work more closely with our Beloved. In the deepest core of the heart, where lover and Beloved are one, God's name is our name. Through the heart, and the knowing of the heart, the Beloved can bring this oneness into life, this imprint of His essential nature into the world.

We are other than God, for God is beyond even our idea of the beyond. And yet we are also one with our Beloved, because there is nothing other than God. The lover knows these not as opposites, but as part of her paradoxical relationship with her Beloved, part of the mystery of love and service. The knowledge of His otherness protects us from inflation, from the ego's identifying itself with God. The experience of oneness enables us to participate more fully in God's revelation, how His oneness is made manifest. Our consciousness of being one with God also enables us to bring His divine essence into the world without the division of duality. This allows the power and majesty of His name, its love and beauty, to work directly with the life of which we are a part.

There is a specific relationship between the fundamental structure of life and God's invisible presence. Divine remembrance can make this relationship known, can make it a part of the consciousness of humanity. Awareness of divine presence can remind the atoms of life that they are included in His divine oneness. When the atoms of life remember their own divinity, there is a shift in their frequency, just as there is a shift in the vibration of a human being when she remembers God. This subtle shift in the fundamental structure of life will release some of the energy hidden within matter. Then we will have to learn how to use this energy, how to work with it for the benefit of all life. This will also have a shadow-side as people will try to use it for personal and selfish motives. But first it is necessary to bring divine remembrance into the physical world, from which it was banished by the fathers of the patriarchy.

To bring divine remembrance into the physical world requires a commitment to life. For the lover there are a deep joy and fulfillment in being here in this world in service to our Beloved. God's name sings in our heart and in our blood. With every step, with every breath, we remember God, and this remembrance is reflected into life. We bring the remembrance of our true nature from the inner recesses of the heart into the physical world. Through our own practice we begin to see how divine oneness is hidden within creation, and our witnessing of this miracle has an effect upon life. Because we carry the consciousness of life, our awareness of the name of God awakens the world to its own deepest knowing of its Creator.

In our cultural drive for sophistication we often overlook the simple power of remembrance. We look for complex answers to our problems, forgetting the primal nature of our existence, life's divine essence. Working with this essence, working with the name of God, we can give creation the potency of conscious remembrance. Divine love can then become alive in a new way; the physical world can turn knowingly upon its axis of love.

The awakening of the world is a science. It is not mystical idealism. Just as the spiritual awakening of a human being follows a careful course, so does this global shift have specific guidelines. We have forgotten the knowledge of how the spiritual and physical dimensions interrelate, how the inner and outer affect each other. For example, there is a specific way to bring the currents of love into matter, just as there is a science in the reflection of light from the inner to the outer. This knowledge is a part of our heritage, and yet it is hidden from us. Ibn 'Arabî expresses this truth:

> God deposited within man knowledge of all things, then prevented him from perceiving what He had deposited within him.... This is one of the divine mysteries which reason denies and considers totally impossible. The nearness of this mystery to those ignorant of it is like God's nearness to His servant, as mentioned in His words, "We are nearer to him than you, but you do not see" (Qur'an 56:85), and His words, "We are nearer to him than his jugular vein" (50:16). In spite of this nearness, the person does not perceive and does not know.... NO ONE KNOWS WHAT IS WITHIN HIMSELF UNTIL IT IS UNVEILED TO HIM INSTANT BY INSTANT.[3]

The unveiling of mystical knowledge is given according to the need of the time. But this unveiling is not performed by a father-figure image of God who acts independent of humanity. Our patriarchal conditioning, in which God is in heaven looking after us, isolates us from the participation that is needed to awaken us to the knowledge that is already present. It is through our witnessing and participation in life that a knowledge is made accessible from within us and within life. The organic relationship among all aspects of life is part of this process. Through our participation in life's organic oneness, the esoteric knowledge of how this oneness functions from a spiritual perspective can be revealed.

Our work is also to be attentive so that we can recognize this knowledge when it is given. Through the remembrance of the heart we are always attentive. We learn to see the signs of God as they are revealed around and within us. Through our inner and outer attention this knowledge can be given to us and to the world. In the last centuries the knowledge that humanity has been given reflects our focus on the physical plane. We have even developed a religion of physical science. The next stage is to bring together the inner and outer, the physical and spiritual dimensions. The knowledge of how they interrelate, how energy flows from the inner to the outer, is crucial if we are to escape our present imbalance.

REALIGNING THE FUNDAMENTAL STRUCTURE OF MATTER

Because humanity carries the divine consciousness of the world, it is through us that this spark of divine consciousness can be reconnected to the physical plane. This process belongs to the feminine mystery of creation. Women carry the divine spark within their physical body; otherwise they would not be able to conceive and give birth. Women are closer to the mystery of matter than men are. They experience the wonder of creation within their body. Even if a woman never becomes pregnant she still has this quality in her cells.

Because our patriarchal culture has separated the spiritual and the physical, one of the first steps in healing the planet is to acknowledge the spiritual potential of matter, to align the world with its divine consciousness. Women can do this work more easily than men can. It is a part of their instinctual spiritual nature. This is one of the reasons that in the West more women than men are attracted to spiritual life—there is a work for which they are needed.

Realigning the structure of matter with divine consciousness will take time. There is a resistance to any such fundamental change. Part of the patriarchal power drive has been to deny matter its magical nature; in this way men could gain power over matter. Traditionally it was the priestesses who understood the magic of nature. This developed from woman's innate understanding of the interrelationship of life, how all of life flows together. Men have a deep fear of woman's magical nature and over the centuries many patterns of repression have been imposed to deny her access to her magical power. These patterns also stand in the way of reawakening matter.

Although it is important to acknowledge the existence of these patterns of repression, we should avoid reconstellating masculine and feminine antagonism. It is vital that we step beyond the dynamic of opposition. The new knowledge that is waiting for us belongs to oneness, and it cannot be accessed if we have an attitude of dualism. Our attitude aligns us with the knowledge that is already present. At any time of transition we need to make sure that we are not caught in patterns of past conflicts. However, we need to acknowledge the existence of these conflicts in order to turn away from their attraction, their magnetic pull and quality of familiarity. Otherwise they affect us in the unconscious where we have less resistance. Masculine and feminine antagonism have deep archetypal roots. We can easily be drawn unknowingly into the battles of previous ages.

Although these patterns of conflict exist, the energy of oneness has a greater power. It is waiting to be lived, to be brought into being. It needs to work through us and come into our relationship with life. And because women have a more instinctual knowing of this oneness, they are needed to reestablish certain connections.

We no longer know how matter speaks to us. We have given our natural knowing into the hands of science and technology. Science has been a significant part of our development, giving us a new understanding of life and the physical world. The next step is to marry this masculine approach with the instinctual knowing of the feminine. We need to combine our scientific knowledge of matter with its magical qualities. This will lead to the science of the future.

However, patriarchal scientific knowledge is so ingrained in our culture and so much a part of our establishment that any change will encounter powerful barriers of resistance. Collectively we believe in science rather than prayer. The simple fact that we have forgotten the power of prayer, or placed it solely within the sphere of personal spirituality, shows the degree to which we have isolated ourself from our spiritual nature. We look for rational answers to our problems rather than working with the divine that is our very core.

How can we give space to a new attitude without engaging in conflict? Prayer and devotion include rather than divide. Prayer does not belong to any institution, but is a direct connection to the one power that is the source of every power. The remembrance of God, the repetition of the divine name, brings the presence of the divine into life. Through our prayer and remembrance the divine can work its magic in the world. It can unveil the knowledge within our hearts, and awaken us to the ways of the future.

A CONSCIOUS STATE OF BEING

The work of the lover is to bring the consciousness of love into the world. This consciousness of love belongs to all of creation, and can be brought into the fundamental structure of life. We carry all levels of creation within us. We also carry within us the blueprint of how all these levels interact. This blueprint is not static, but a constantly changing and evolving process, although it does follow certain laws. These laws are the spiritual guiding principles of humanity and of all life forms on this planet. They are not separate from creation but are a part of cellular structure and its DNA. It is our ability to read, understand, and enact these laws, these principles of life, that determines the well-being of life and the whole body of the planet. When we transgress these laws, we create an imbalance. It is not that we are punished by a judgmental God, but that we go against the natural way, what Chinese sages called the Tao.

The Tao is life in its essential nature, "the mother of the ten thousand things." Its principles belong to the balance of life:

> The mother principle of ruling holds good for a long time.
> This is called having deep roots and a firm foundation,
> The Tao of long life and eternal vision.[4]

When life loses its harmony we suffer. When we lose our "deep roots and firm foundation" we are easily thrown off balance. As life evolves there are subtle shifts in the way the principles of balance and harmony enact themselves, and part of the work of those committed to spiritual service is to realign life with these shifts. One aspect of this work is done through love. Because love belongs to the core of our being and to all of life, it can flow directly to the heart of matter. Through our participation in life we can bring His love directly into the physical plane, even into the movement of its atoms. Love can be used to realign life, to reconnect life to its natural state of balance and harmony.

This natural state of being belongs to all levels of life. It is not a static state, but evolves according to the shifts in the principles that govern creation. Because our masculine focus is on action and "doing," we look for new ways to act to solve our problems. We overlook the feminine principle of "being" and the need to find a new way to "be." The "doing" capacity has been instilled in us through our parents and so many aspects of our culture. To return to our "deep roots and a firm foundation" in our natural state of being, we need to translate it into "being" instead.

There is a consciousness to "being" that needs to be included in life, a quality of attention that connects the higher and lower, the inner and outer. We know this attention, this inner state of being, in our meditation and prayer. In inner silence we wait, attentive to what comes from our higher nature. To bring this attitude into our outer, physical life is a challenge, particularly when there is such pressure to act rather than "be." But without this state of conscious being, life will lose its balance; the energy that is coming into creation will not flow into the new channels that have been prepared.

Presence, attention, witnessing are spiritual practices that belong to an awakened state of being. They enable our consciousness to participate directly with the flow of life. Inwardly we are attentive to the principles of life, to the unwritten laws of creation. Outwardly we reflect these principles into manifestation through our attitude and the way we live. This way, the flow of outer life can follow the patterns of change that are happening within. Because we have been so focused on outer action, we have lost the knowledge of how the energy of life can be directed by our attention. A conscious state of being in which the inner and outer are in harmony is a powerful force in the world.

When energy flows freely from the inner to the outer, a new dynamic in life can manifest. The fundamental structure of life will shift in a very subtle way; its axis will change, and this will enable part of its energetic potential to be realized. At the moment, our collective attitude imprisons this energy in matter. This imprisonment is reflected in our present science, which requires that we use force to release the energy in matter in the volatile and dangerous form of nuclear energy.

But when there is a balanced flow between the inner and outer, matter can respond and release its energy freely. Part of this process concerns the dynamic interrelationship of consciousness and energy and matter, which has been suggested by particle physics.[5] Physicists working at the sub-atomic level of matter have noted that the attitude of the observer has a direct effect on the way the energy of matter appears to act. This interface of consciousness and energy will be an important area of future scientific progress. There are ways to work with the energy of matter that are only at the threshold of our awareness, and other ways that at present remain hidden.

Mystics know the ways energy and light can be directed by our attention. Through real attention to daily life we bring awareness and the light of the soul into the outer world. This is described in the Naqshbandi Sufi practice of "Attentiveness," (*nigah dasht*). "Be always mindful of what you are thinking and doing so you may put the imprint of your immortality on every passing incident and instance of your daily life." Also, in our practice of the *dhikr* we can bring the name of God into the world of matter—for example, repeating the divine name while we cook infuses the food with the energy and love of remembrance. One could taste the love in my teacher's cooking!

Working on the inner planes, through our inner attention, we reflect light and love where they are needed. We can also focus the name of God into the diffuse energy of the uncreated, and use our attention to unblock energy so that it can flow into manifestation.

Other ways to work with the energy of matter will also become available. What we call "magic" is a variety of ways to work with matter on an energetic level, and there are different levels of magic, different ways to work with the energy of creation.[6] This is all a part of the science of how the inner and outer relate. Consciousness and matter are not isolated from each other. When we begin to understand the interdependent oneness of creation and how the different levels of reality are connected, different fields of knowledge will become accessible.

THE ANGER OF THE EARTH

We need to be careful at this time of transition. Matter is not as static or as solid as we perceive. We do not know that the energy within matter can become wrathful, that it can turn against us. In China the earth energy was imaged as dragon, whose power was to be respected. There are forces within the physical world that we do not understand. There are also forces which until now have been dormant, but could easily awaken.

Psychology has shown us that we have unwelcome forces in our personal and collective psyches which can be very destructive when they awake and come to the surface. We know that anger can arise from the feeling of being mistreated or abused, and that this power of vengeance exists on both a personal and collective level. But we have little understanding of how such forces can exist within matter, how its dragon-energy could erupt. We are ignorant and arrogant in our relationship to the physical world. We continue to abuse it without real concern for any consequences.

As the energy patterns in the world begin to change, more energy will flow to the surface. The free flow of energy around the world that we experience in the global marketplace and in global communication is an aspect of this shift, but these energetic changes are not happening only on the surface level of business and technology. Something within the core of the world is awakening and making its presence felt. A certain barrier that had defined the physical dimension and held it apart from the energies of the inner world is falling away. This has to do with the merging of the inner and outer, the coming together of these two dimensions.

In our dualistic thinking we forget that a shift in our collective consciousness also means a shift in the earth's energy. Our science may measure the ecological effects of pollution, climate changes, and global warming, but we do not understand the relationship between our consciousness and the earth. We do not realize that there can be a direct energetic relationship between our collective consciousness and the earth's energy patterns.

Responsibility for our planet becomes a central theme as we move into a new era. We need to become more aware of how our attitudes, which are polluting and violating the earth, can disrupt the balance of life. This is not just primitive superstition, but an understanding of the way energy flows in the physical world. In many cultures the work of shamans was to heal any imbalance that we might create in the web of life. To quote Martin Prechtel,

> Shamans are sometimes considered healers or doctors, but really they are people who deal with the tears and holes we create in the net of life, the damage that we all cause in our search for survival.[7]

We may be aware of the danger of earthquakes and climate changes, but we have forgotten that the earth can be angry. We do not have enough shamans to repair any imbalance we have created. We do not know how to work with the energy structure of the world. And these patterns of energy are changing, just as our collective consciousness is shifting.

The heart contains a direct connection to the energy structure of the planet and the ways the energy flows. The heart *chakra* is the center of the human being, the home of the Self which contains the consciousness of the whole. Because the human being is linked with the whole of creation, the heart gives us access to its energy. The consciousness of the heart can make a real contribution to the balance and flow of the energy of matter. As this energy becomes more awake and active, His lovers are helping to balance it. Like the shamans of previous times, they are working to counter the negative effect of corporate greed and other forces that seek only to exploit the physical world. On a more subtle level they are learning to work with the energy of matter so that its potential can be used beneficially, rather than in the destructive dynamic of chaos.

Until recently, mystics have mainly worked on the inner planes. But the shift in the energy structure of the planet is turning our attention to the physical plane. At the present this work is in its infancy, but the changes that are taking place require careful attention. Through our attention the awakening energy of the world can flow in a beneficial manner, create the riverbeds that belong to the flow of life in the future.

A MULTIDIMENSIONAL APPROACH

The changes taking place in our world are so new and so profound that we do not have a model in our recent history to help us understand or relate to them. The shifts in the energy structure of the planet are beyond our immediate comprehension. The possibility that the energy of matter could awaken seems pure fantasy. And yet particle physics has prepared us for a paradigm totally different from our present relationship to the physical world. To accept that our consciousness and the world of matter could have a direct interrelationship requires a degree of responsibility we are reluctant to take. But if we do not take this step, the energy that is being awakened could become very destructive.

In past ages mystics and shamans have guided humanity at times of transition. One of the fathers of our Western civilization, the ancient Greek philosopher Parmenides, was a mystic. Through his connection to the inner worlds he brought justice and law-giving, and laid the foundation for much of our culture.[8] Present Western culture does not honor its mystics, but they are still present among us. Because their work has been primarily on the inner planes, the lack of external recognition has not mattered to them; rather it has enabled them to continue their work without disturbance. But if a certain esoteric knowledge is to be given to humanity, there needs to be a recognition of the tradition of real knowledge and wisdom coming from within.

How do we know what is fantasy and what is truth? The physical world is more strange than it may appear or than we would like to believe. And, as Rûmî reminds us, mystics exist in a paradoxical, crazy reality that is passionately alive:

> Oh daylight arise! Atoms are dancing,
> Souls lost in ecstasy, are dancing....
> They are all like madmen; each atom, happy or miserable,
> Is passionate for the Sun of which nothing can be said.[9]

Within the heart different worlds coexist, bonded by the oneness of love. The knowledge we need is not separate from us. It is our heritage and also a gift. The earth is alive because everything is alive; "every created atom is articulate with love." Our consciousness does not need to be limited to a reality defined by physical form. It can see what is hidden within matter, know what is hidden within the heart.

But the radical potential of what is being given at this time requires that we step away from our old ways of understanding and perceiving the world. The knowledge of the past has become inadequate. Developments in technology have prepared us for a changing world, one that is more interconnected than we knew even a decade ago. But this is only the beginning of a fundamental realignment that demands our careful attention. The interconnectedness of the inner and outer will take us into a very different world.

We do not understand the physical effects of our collective consciousness. We abuse the earth mentally as well as physically, with no recognition that there could be any consequences. Nor do we understand that the physical pollution of the planet affects us mentally, psychologically, and even spiritually. But once we realize that all of life interrelates not only on a physical level, but across different levels of reality, we will have to embrace a multidimensional awareness.

As this era of masculine dominance comes to an end and a feminine understanding of life's wholeness is included, we are beginning to experience a different world in which physical, mental, and spiritual well-being are interdependent. We see the signs of this in the new age movement. But the new age movement is often limited by its focus on individual well-being. Our real concern is the well-being of the planet and the whole of humanity. Central to this is the understanding that the physical world cannot be healed from a solely physical perspective, but requires a shift to an attitude that contains a multidimensional approach.

Once we make a conscious decision to be open to this vaster, less defined world, life will respond. Life cannot connect with our consciousness until we take this step. The created world has much to teach us, but it needs our conscious cooperation and participation as part of its living organism. If we approach life as separate, we will only see the reflection of our dysfunctionalism. If we approach life from the perspective of oneness, it will reveal the wonder and magic that will help us to heal the wounds we have inflicted upon ourself and our world. The physical world will also teach us how to release the energy it has within it, and how to bring this energy to fruition.

Matter is spinning and dancing with the same love that radiates in our soul. The spinning of the heart and the spinning of atoms belong to the same outpouring of love. The power of love and the energy of matter come from the same source. The web of life is a single outpouring of joy that is becoming conscious in a new way. Life needs us not only to help heal its wounds but to celebrate its awakening. Praise and prayer can align the world with its axis of love, where this celebration has begun.

> Each atom hides beneath its veil
> The soul-amazing beauty of the Beloved's Face.[10]

This beauty is being revealed afresh. If we knew the wonder of this moment, we would become instantly intoxicated. The world may cover us with its appearance of problems, but the love, joy, and wisdom that are being born belong to a different vibration. Through our consciousness this vibration can be infused into matter. Our consciousness can then be linked with the soul of matter and we can work directly with its energy structure. This synergy of consciousness and matter is a gift of our future.

The World Soul is not just a psychological
or philosophical concept. It is a living spiritual substance
within us and around us. Just as the individual soul pervades
the whole human being — our body, thoughts, and feelings —
the nature of the World Soul is that it is present
within everything. It pervades all of creation,
and is a unifying principle
within the world.

At the present time our collective culture
sees life primarily from a material perspective —
we worship the god of consumerism, making acquisition
our life's goal. We are imprisoned within matter. We have
forgotten the symbolic and sacred meaning of the outer world.
Alienated from our soul, we have alienated creation
from its deeper meaning. And because we have
denied the world its divinity,
it is slowly dying.

8

Anima Mundi:
Awakening the Soul of the World

God redeems humanity, but nature needs to be redeemed
by human alchemists, who are able to induce the process of
transformation, which alone is capable of liberating
the light imprisoned in physical creation.
STEPHAN HOELLER[1]

The world is a living spiritual being. This was understood by
the ancient philosophers and the alchemists who referred to
the spiritual essence of the world as the *anima mundi*, the "Soul
of the World." They regarded the World Soul as a pure ethereal
spirit diffused throughout all nature, the divine essence that
embraces and energizes all life in the universe.

Throughout history our understanding of the world as a
living being with a spiritual essence has dramatically changed.
Plato understood that "the cosmos is a single Living Creature
which contains all living creatures within it."[2] While this tradition was carried on by the Gnostics and later the alchemists,
the Church fathers imaged a world that was neither divine nor
sacred. A transcendent divinity was the source of all creation,
and humanity lived in exile from heaven in a state of sin. This
doctrine created a split between matter and spirit, causing the
world to be seen as separate from its Creator.

The understanding of the world as sacred resurfaced from
time to time over the next centuries. In the Gothic movement

of the twelfth century, and later in the Renaissance, the created world was briefly seen through the image of the World Soul. In their cathedrals the Gothic architects reflected their vision of a sacred order within creation that belongs to this feminine divine principle. The World Soul animated and formed nature according to divine proportions, which the architects, masons, sculptors, and stained-glass artists imaged in their creations.[3]

Again during the Renaissance nature was briefly seen as a living spiritual essence:

> If medieval theology had removed God to a wholly transcendent sphere, to the Renaissance Platonists nature was permeated by life, divinity, and numinous mystery, a vital expression of the World Soul and the living powers of creation. In the words of Richard Tarnas, "The garden of the world was again enchanted, with magical powers and transcendent meaning implicit in every part of nature."[4]

In the Renaissance the World Soul was understood as a spiritual essence within creation, guiding the unfolding of life and the cosmos. In the words of the Renaissance philosopher Giordano Bruno, the World Soul "illumines the universe and directs nature in producing her species in the right way."[5] The World Soul was also the creative principle that the Renaissance artists sought to channel in their work. Their art was based upon the same sacred proportions they saw in nature, and they understood the imagination as a magical power that can "lure and channel the energies of the *anima mundi.*"

The Renaissance left us great wonders of art and the imagination. It was a brief flowering, however. The orthodoxies of the Church reestablished the split between matter and spirit, and the rise of science began to image the natural world as a machine whose disembodied workings human beings could rationally understand and master. The magical world of creative mystery infused with divine spirit became a dream belonging only to poets and the laboratories and symbolic writings of the alchemists.

The alchemists continued to explore the *anima mundi*. While the Church looked for light in the heavens, the alchemists sought the light hidden in matter. They understood that there was a sacred essence in the fabric of creation, which through their experiments and imagination they worked to release. For the alchemists the *anima mundi* is the divine spark in matter, the "philosophical Mercury," which is the "universal and scintillating fire in the light of nature, which carries the heavenly spirit with it."

Alchemy is concerned with turning lead into gold, liberating the light hidden in the darkness—"the fiery sparks of the world soul, i.e. the light of nature ... dispersed or sprinkled throughout the structure of the great world into all fruits of the elements everywhere."[6] The alchemists also understood that there is a connection between the *anima mundi* and the soul or innermost secret of man. The source of the wisdom and knowledge of the all-pervading essence of the *anima mundi* was "the inner-most and most secret *numinosum* of man."[7]

In the last century Carl Jung rediscovered the wisdom of the alchemical *opus* and showed how alchemical symbols image the process of inner transformation that can release this hidden light. Jung differentiated between two forms of spiritual light: *lumen dei*, the light proceeding from the spiritual realm of a transcendent God, and *lumen naturae*, the light hidden in matter and the forces of nature. The Divine Light may be experienced through revelation and spiritual practices that give us access to our transcendent self. The Light of Nature needs to be released through inner alchemy so that it can work creatively in the world.

The tradition of alchemy reinterpreted into the language of inner transformation is a key to help us to liberate our natural light and to transform the world. The alchemical light hidden in darkness is our own light, which is also the divine spark within matter. Our natural light is part of the light of the World Soul. This alchemical unlocking of matter can be associated with freeing, or awakening, the World Soul, the *anima mundi*. As a microcosm of the whole, the individual can participate directly in the alchemical process that liberates this light, a light that is needed to understand the mysteries of creation and the ways of working with its magical nature. With the *lumen naturae* we can once again learn how to unlock the secrets of nature, so that we no longer have to attack and destroy the natural world in order to survive.

Alchemy is our Western tradition of inner transformation. Sufis have always known about the inner process of alchemy.[8] One of the early Sufi masters, Dhû'l-Nûn, was described as an alchemist, and a great twelfth-century Sufi, al-Ghazzalî, titled one of his most important books *The Alchemy of Happiness*. Sufis have mastered the alchemy of the heart, through which the energy of love transforms the individual to reveal the light hidden within the darkness of the *nafs* or lower self. They developed a detailed science for working with the chambers of the heart to effect an inner transformation that gives the wayfarer access to the light of his true nature. This work does not belong just to the individual, but can have a direct relationship to the whole of creation and the heart of the world. Once we recognize the mysterious connection between our own innermost essence and the soul of the world, we can use the tools of inner transformation to work directly with the soul of the world, to help the *anima mundi* reveal its divine light and awaken.

AS ABOVE SO BELOW

As a result of Jung's writings on alchemy, we have begun to understand the nature of the inner alchemical work. The work on the alchemical lead—the *prima materia*, that which is "glorious and vile, precious and of small account and is found everywhere"[9]—is the work on the shadow, the rejected and unacknowledged parts of our psyche. The philosopher's stone, the gold made from the lead, is our own true nature, the Self. Rather than a transcendent, disembodied divinity, alchemy reveals a divine light that exists in the very depths of our psyche. This light hidden in darkness, the *lumen naturae*, is also our instinctual self and natural way of being, which until it is revealed is covered over by patterns of conditioning and the layers of the false self.

What is the difference between the light discovered in the depths of the psyche and the light of our transcendent divine Self glimpsed in meditation or other experiences? *It is the same light*, experienced in different ways. The Sufis know that the Beloved, the source of all light, has both an immanent and a transcendent quality. The Beloved whom we love is both "nearer to him than his jugular vein" and "beyond even his idea of the beyond." The Self, "larger than large and smaller than small," has the same dual quality.

The yogi deep in meditation and the alchemist in his laboratory are seeking the same light, the same divine nature. Everything that we experience has a dual nature, a masculine and a feminine aspect, and the same is true of the light of the Self. It can be experienced in its masculine form as a pure transcendent light, consciousness without the constrictions of the psyche or the physical world. In meditation we can first glimpse and then rest in our eternal and infinite nature, and come to know a reality not defined or constricted by our body or the manifest world. This is a reality of light upon light, our colorless and formless essence.

We can also come to know our divine nature in its feminine, embodied nature, as the light of being, our natural wisdom, the gold of our true nature. In this light we experience and know the divine within creation, the way our Beloved reveals Himself in a multitude of forms, each form a different expression of His infinite being. We see how each color, each smell, every taste, even every thought and feeling, is a unique expression of the divine. In this way we come to know God in His creation in a way that is hidden in the transcendent. In this revelation we see that each thing is unique and that all things are one, and we discover the relationship of the parts to the whole—the interconnected wonder of creation. We see the rich tapestry of life and know that it is one Being revealing Itself in so many ways.

If we are not to remain in the paradigm of duality, living our inherited split between masculine and feminine, spirit and matter, we need to acknowledge both of these aspects. We cannot afford to follow the footsteps of the patriarchal Church fathers and seek only a transcendent light, look only towards heaven. We also need to know the light hidden in matter and understand the magic of creation that it reveals. We need to know the mysteries of creation as celebrated in the most sacred text of the alchemists, the *Emerald Tablet*, attributed to Hermes Trismegistos:

> What is below is like that which is above, and what is above is like that which is below, to accomplish the miracles of the one thing.[10]

The light hidden in matter is the one light experienced within the mystery of creation, the hidden treasure revealed through the dance of multiplicity. The creation of the manifest world is a revelation of the hidden nature of the divine, as expressed in the *hadîth*, "I was a hidden treasure and I longed to be known, so I created the world." But we can only experience the wonder and know the true nature of this revelation through the light hidden within it. Just as He has hidden His secret within us—"Man is My secret and I am his secret"—so has He hidden Himself within His creation. Sometimes, in moments amidst the beauty or glory of nature, in the vastness of the stars or the perfection of the early morning dew on a flower, we glimpse this wonder. The light hidden in matter breaks through and we stand in awe before our Creator, as reflected in the words of the poet Gerard Manley Hopkins:

> The world is charged with the grandeur of God.
> It will flame out, like shining from shook foil. [11]

Through this light we can awaken to the divine nature of life and experience the real beauty of His revelation. There is only one light—"as above so below"—and yet in His creation

He reveals Himself in a way that is not revealed by His transcendent light, the *lumen dei*. What is true for the Creator is also true for us who are "made in His image." The light that is discovered in the depths of the psyche, through the work on the shadow and the inner alchemical *opus*, reveals part of our divine nature that is hidden from a purely transcendent consciousness. We come to know ourself and our Beloved in a new way. For each of us this revelation is unique. Part of the wonder of creation is how she offers a different experience to each of us; even the same apple tasted by two people will be a different experience. Through the light of the divine we can see life as it really is, in the uniqueness of our own experience of it and not just through the veils of our projections, and so taste the divine uniqueness of each moment. At the same time we experience this uniqueness as part of a greater oneness. We see the threads that connect together all of life; we see how each part reflects the whole.

> Whoever can't see the whole in every part plays at
>   blind man's bluff;
> A wise man tastes the Tigris in every sip.[12]

CONNECTIONS OF LIGHT

In our deeper knowing we understand this deep connectedness of all of life. And yet the Church, the rise of Western science, and a growing culture of materialism have effectively banished the *anima mundi* from our collective imagination, until, in the words of Jung, "man himself has ceased to be the microcosm and his anima is no longer the consubstantial *scintilla* or spark of the *Anima Mundi*, the World Soul."[13] How can we redeem this relationship, recreate this connection in our imagination and inner work? How can we return our light to the World Soul?

Once we make the simple acknowledgment that we are a part of the whole, then a connection is made between our light and the world. We make this connection with our consciousness and with our imagination; then through this connection our light begins to flow. In this way we begin to redeem the work of the whole. These connections create pathways of light that find their way through the darkness of the collective psyche. Just as in our personal psyche, there are blocks and places of resistance to this flow of light, and there are also places of power, creativity, and unexpected qualities.

The World Soul is not a fixed or defined substance, but a living substance made out of the hopes, dreams, and deepest imaginings of humanity and of all creation. This is the home of creation's collective memories and the myths of humanity. Here are the archetypes and powers that define our life. Here are hidden places of magical meaning, places where dreams can come into being. We have lived for so long in the stark barrenness of a rational landscape that we have forgotten the potency that lies beneath the surface. Flowing through the pathways created by our conscious connection to the *anima mundi*, our light will find its way to places of power that are within the world, places where deeper layers of meaning are waiting to come alive.

We presently see the material world as something apart from ourselves, a solid and enduring object without life or magic. Like the seventeenth-century scientists who decided animals had no feelings and thus could be dissected without suffering, we feel free to inflict our will upon our world, pillaging it for our own gain without any thought to the suffering and damage we are subjecting it to. Caught up in our materialistic drives, we may not recognize that this image of the world is an illusion, an insubstantial dream that can easily alter or dissolve as new forces come into play. As our light makes its connections within the World Soul, it will activate some of these forces, energies that are waiting to liberate the world from this destructive illusion. We know how this works in our own alchemical journey, how what we find beneath the surface changes our values in unexpected ways, how connections are then made and synchronicities occur that before would have been unbelievable. As we make these connections, we will begin to see that both the world and our own selves are more magical than we know.

This work of connecting our light to the world does not need to be done through a mass movement, or by millions of people. For centuries a few alchemists held these secrets of inner transformation against the powerful forces of the Church and establishment. The real work is always done by a small number of individuals. What matters is the level of participation: whether we dare to make a real commitment to the work of the soul. Unlike the alchemists living in their laboratories, we do not need to give up our ordinary outer life—everyday life can also be a necessary balance and protection against the strange delusions so easily created by the inner world. But we do need to recognize that there is a certain work that needs to be done, and that we can no longer stand on the sidelines and watch our collective dreams spin out of control.

Our culture may have isolated us within our individual self, separated us from the magic of life—but once again this is just a surface mirage. We are all connected and part of the living substance of creation. Within every cell of our being, every spark of consciousness, we have a knowing of oneness. Our own inner journey cannot be separate from the journey of the whole. An inner journey separate from the whole is no real journey; it is just another illusion created by an ego that wants to protect itself.

The substance of our soul is part of the fabric of life, the tapestry of creation in which are woven the unicorns and monsters of our dreams as well as the skyscrapers of our cities. The inner and outer worlds are not separate—despite all the efforts of our rational culture to have us believe they are. The recent dramas of terrorism have once again brought demons into our living rooms, and we sense there is nowhere really safe from these shadows. But we do not need to simply be victims of these archetypal nightmares. By evoking the real magic that comes from within, we can work to balance the light and the dark, and creatively participate in changing the dreams that define our collective life.

The light of the World Soul is waiting to be used to connect us with the inner powers that belong to matter and to life itself. The real world is an enchanted place, full of magical powers waiting to be used. And, as the alchemists understood, the *anima mundi* is a creative force: "it is the artist, the craftsperson, the 'inner Vision' which shapes and differentiates the prime matter, giving it form."[14]

AWAKENING TO THE PURPOSE OF CREATION

The World Soul is not just a psychological or philosophical concept. It is a living spiritual substance within us and around us. Just as the individual soul pervades the whole human being—our body, thoughts, and feelings—the nature of the

World Soul is that it is present within everything. It pervades all of creation, and is a unifying principle within the world. The alchemist-physician Thomas Browne saw it as "the Universal Spirit of Nature, the *anima mundi* or World-Soul responsible for all phenomena and which binds all life together."[15] Marsilio Ficino saw the World Soul flourishing everywhere:

> The soul is all things together.... And since it is the center of all things, it has the forces of all. Hence it passes into all things. And since it is the true connection of all things, it goes to the one without leaving the others. ... therefore it may rightly be called the center of nature, the middle term of all things, the face of all, the bond and juncture of the universe.[16]

The soul of the world permeates all of creation like salt in water. The physical world is the denser plane, and within it and sustaining it is the reality of the soul, which contains the Higher Intelligence that is the creative and ordering principle of life.

This divine intelligence is in everything. It is the spark within matter, the light within a human being. When we isolate ourself from our own soul, we deny ourself conscious access to this light, to its guidance and intelligence. Then our life becomes without meaning or purpose, "a walking shadow ... signifying nothing." Without real purpose, our life is just a physical existence. When we reconnect with our soul, the magic and meaning of life come alive both within us and around us.

Our real gift to life is an awareness of its purpose. When we are aware of life's purpose, the light of the soul shines in our life, and its secret hidden within the world comes alive. And the light that is within us is within everything; it is "at the center of all things." When our light comes alive within us, it comes alive within all of creation. It reveals to creation its true purpose. At the present time our collective culture sees life primarily from a material perspective—we worship the god of consumerism, making acquisition our life's goal. We are imprisoned within matter. We have forgotten the symbolic and sacred meaning of the outer world. Alienated from our soul, we have alienated creation from its deeper meaning. And because we have denied the world its divinity, it is slowly dying.

The real alchemical work is to liberate creation from this imprisonment—to awaken life to its meaning. We have to free the light that is within us and within the world. A transcendent image of the divine will only give us access to a transcendent light. We need the light hidden in matter, the gold that is within lead. When this light comes alive within life, it can change the patterns of creation and create the forms of the future that will bring life back into harmony. It can manifest its unifying nature.

The alchemists understood the nature of this light:

> It is the father of every miraculous work in the whole
> world....
> Its power is perfect if it is converted to earth.[17]

Working within the world, this power is the light and power of the divine made manifest. The light that is within our own psyche is the light within the *anima mundi*. In the depth of ourself we discover this essential oneness. This is the same awareness as the yogi's realization that one's true nature and unchanging self (*atman*) is the Universal Self (*Atman*). What is within us is within everything. Once we understand this truth, we step outside of the parameters of our individual self and come to realize the power that is within us. This shift in awareness is a very simple step that has profound consequences.

IMAGINING THE WORLD

At the moment, the world is asleep, suffering the dreams of humanity, which have become a nightmare of desecration and pollution. In our hubris we have forgotten that the world is more than our collective projections, that it is more mysterious and strange than our rational minds would like us to believe. Quantum physics has revealed a fluid and unpredictable world, in which consciousness and matter are not separate—whether a photon of light behaves as a particle or wave depends upon the consciousness of the observer. But we remain within the images of Newtonian physics: matter that is dead, definable, and solid, and consciousness that is objective, safely divorced from the physical world. Matter and spirit remain split, and we continue in the patriarchal fantasy that we can have control over our world.

As we have already seen, the physical world was not always experienced as so isolated. Many cultures have been more concerned with the relationship between the worlds. In the medieval imagination the physical world was just one part of the Great Chain of Being. Medieval cathedrals imaged a symbolic and geometric relationship between the different parts, with the maze that symbolized our journey through this world mirroring the rose window's image of a higher reality of light. In the Sufism of Ibn 'Arabî, the worlds were seen as connected by the symbolic world of the imagination, which acts as a bridge or an "intermediary between the world of Mystery (*'alam al-ghayb*) and the world of Visibility (*'alam al-shahadat*)."

In their retorts and crucibles the alchemists were working not just with chemical substances but also with the inner energies of life. Their symbolic writings describe both the mixture of tinctures and the marriage of the king and queen, the union of sun and moon. The alchemists took their work seriously, knowing the real responsibility involved.[18] They knew that they were working with a secret substance in life, "mercury" or "quicksilver," a catalyst that can transform whatever it touches. The way their chemicals changed and transformed imaged how life can be changed with the correct mixture of ingredients. They knew that matter and spirit are not separate. Modern science is now revealing the same thing to us. Yet how the inner and outer worlds relate, and how our consciousness affects the physical world, remain for us still a great mystery.

Once we surrender our safe concept of a separate, static, and defined world, we open to a more dynamic reality in which life is an energy field with which our consciousness and unconscious interact: a pulsating Indra's Net being continually woven by the soul, through which our consciousness takes on form, our dreams come into being.

LIBERATING THE ANIMA MUNDI

We need the magical powers within nature in order to heal and transform our world. But awakening these powers would mean that our patriarchal institutions will lose their control, as once again the mysterious inner world will come into play, releasing forces once understood and used by the priestess and the shaman, whose existence the patriarchal world has forgotten. The science of the future will work with these forces, exploring how the different worlds interrelate, including how the energies of the inner can be used in the outer. The shaman and the scientist will work together, the wisdom of the priestess and wisdom of the physician renew their ancient connection.

But the first step is to awaken these powers, not just individually but for the whole world. We are moving into a global era, and any real changes need to be made globally. If we try to grasp powers for our own individual use, we risk descending into black magic, which is the use of inner powers for the purposes of the ego. Our next step in evolution is to realize the primal truth of oneness and to reunite our individual light with the whole.

The work pioneered by Jung has given us access to the science of alchemy, revealing this hidden part of our Western esoteric tradition. Psychological techniques have been developed to help reveal an inner world of energy, power, and creative potential. We no longer need to stay locked in the surface world. But our tendency has been to take this access for our individual selves, our own inner journey, and not realize its larger implications.

Real alchemical work was always for the sake of the whole. In our inner journey, our own alchemical process, to work for the sake of the whole means to acknowledge the dimension of the *anima mundi*. The light we discover in our own depths is a spark of the World Soul, and the world needs this light in order to evolve. When we make this connection in our consciousness and our imagination, we begin to change the fabric of life. The alchemists knew the potency of this spark, this philosophical mercury. The same substance that transforms our individual self is the primordial world-creating spirit, the "universal and scintillating fire in the light of nature, which carries the heavenly spirit with it." When we liberate it within ourselves but do not claim it just for ourselves, solely for our own inner process, we create certain connections through which this energy can flow into the core of life. We participate in the alchemical work of liberating the *anima mundi*. This is the first step in the work.

What does it really mean, to liberate the *anima mundi*? In our individual alchemical *opus* we experience the effects of freeing the light, energy, and creative potential that lie within us. We know how this liberation can radically change our vision and experience of life. We are taken into a different dimension of our self, and life begins to magically open doors that before were closed or hidden. Of course these changes are not always what we may want—they do not fulfill our surface desires, but they have a deeper meaning and purpose. Something within us awakens and the life of the spirit begins. The alchemists understood that the individual is a microcosm of the whole, and that what can happen to each of us can happen to the world.

When the light of the soul returns, a grey world of drudgery begins to sparkle; the multihued qualities of creation become visible. Instead of the endless pursuit of pleasure, life beckons us on a search for meaning: the colors of life speak to us, telling us their story, singing to us their song. The music of life returns, a music that is creation alive. A real dialogue between our inner self and our outer life begins to unfold as we directly participate in the hidden mystery of life coming alive: it comes alive within ourself and within the world. In the light of the soul the barriers between inner and outer dissolve, and we no longer have to dig beneath the surface for some semblance of purpose to our lives.

The light of the soul returning to the *anima mundi* will free us from the stranglehold of materialism, because it will awaken us to different qualities within life, give us different dreams to follow. In this light we will see life differently; a different world will become visible. When matter is dead and the soul is asleep, we are easily seduced by the attractions of materialism: we see nothing else to fulfill us. But we know in our own journey how we can suddenly be awakened to a different reality that was always around us and yet hidden from sight, a world that does not belong to buying and selling but to the mystery of the soul. Then a sense of wonder and awe returns. The same can happen with the world. We are longing to participate in a life that is multidimensional and full of beauty rather than just pursuing our own pleasure. Who would not turn from lust to love? The light of the soul is the spirit within matter that makes life dance. It awakens us to the simple joy of what is:

> i thank You God for most this amazing
> day:for the leaping greenly spirits of trees
> and a blue true dream of sky;and for everything
> which is natural which is infinite which is yes
>
> (i who have died am alive again today,
> and this is the sun's birthday;this is the birth
> day of life and of love and wings:and of the gay
> great happening illimitably earth)[19]

This is the world into which we were born. Even our city streets and shopping malls are alive in a way that is presently veiled. Creation is sparkling in so many ways, though its spectrum of colors is at present only partly visible. We have created a prison of materialism, but it is just an illusion. If we let life speak to us, it will show us the way to unlock this door, pull down these walls, dissolve this nightmare. There are forces within life more powerful than our corporations and politicians. And these forces do not play by the rules we have created. With laughter and a glint of mischief, they can rearrange our lives.

Our world is presently asleep. Its magical powers are for the most part dormant, but they are present, waiting to be used to transform our world. We have confined miracles to the safety of small events, but the whole world is miraculous. We may talk about the "miracle of life," but we place this miracle within the safe container of what we expect to happen. We do not dare to recognize that a real miracle is the unexpected, the divine waking up in life. We may try to block off this dimension that is pure joy and light, to remain within the confines of our egos and expectations. But to do that is to deny the divinity of creation, deny that there is an Intelligence continually recreating the world according to divine principles that are beyond our rational understanding.

On our individual inner journey we begin to glimpse the workings of our soul, how it helps to create our outer life in an often miraculous way, as well as rearranging our inner selves. As we turn away from the ego towards the soul, we see more of its power and purpose. Its light is the ordering principle in our lives; it can create harmony out of the disparate aspects of our psyche, bring the mandala of the Self into being. Through the workings of the soul we begin to have an outer life in balance with our inner self. It is no different for the world. The *anima mundi* is the ordering and creative principle in creation. Without her presence we experience only the fractious elements of our egos—the greed, insecurity, and power dynamics that are so visible in our contemporary landscape. When her light is awakened, then she can bring the world into harmony and balance. This simple and radical truth was known to the alchemists: it is the light hidden in matter that will redeem the world.

*... the first step is to acknowledge that the
world is a spiritual being, just as you acknowledge
for yourself that you are a spiritual being. And the
next is to recognize the mysterious relationship
between the individual and the world, known
traditionally as microcosm and macrocosm,
in which every human being is the
microcosm of the
whole.*

*... we have a problem now. The world is dying.
It is not supposed to be like this. I am convinced that
human beings are not meant to sit looking at a flickering
screen ten hours a day pressing buttons. Human beings are
so extraordinary! They are full of light; they have this
divine intelligence. They are meant to live in a
sacred way, not spend their life looking at a
flickering television or computer screen.
That is not what we were
created for.*

9

Invoking the World Soul

*Transcript of a talk given May, 2007
in Seattle, Washington*

What I want to talk about this evening is the *anima mundi*—
the soul of the world. This is the living spirit of creation, the
divine consciousness within matter. In fact I don't want to just
talk about the *anima mundi*; I want to see if we can invoke Her
presence.

I will begin by just giving a little history of the *anima mundi*
in our Western culture. In the East, the *anima mundi* is very
evident. The Tao, for example—it's the same thing—is the divine within creation; Taoism is really a constant relationship
to that living spirit in nature, in which one aligns one's whole
life, one's whole way of being, one's whole understanding of
life, in relationship to this living spirit. In the West we have a
more conceptual understanding of it. This is the tradition of
what we call now the Gaia Principle—the understanding that
the earth is a living being. And all I would add at the beginning
in order to understand this and to relate to it is that it is a living
spiritual being. And just as *we* are a physical body with a soul,
so is the world a physical body with a soul, and that soul *is* its

spiritual essence. And as far as I can understand, unless you make a relationship to the soul of creation, the *anima mundi*, you are just scratching the surface of life, just as somebody who relates to you purely physically is just scratching your surface, not relating to you as a living breathing spiritual being, a soul incarnate in this world.

One can go back, for example, to Plato who understood the cosmos as a single living creature that contains all living creatures within it. So at the very origins of our Western civilization there is this deep understanding that the earth is a living spiritual being. Later there were the alchemists who regarded the World Soul as a pure ethereal spirit diffused throughout all nature, the divine essence that infuses and energizes all life in the universe. So the *anima mundi* is this living spiritual—not just principle, but substance, within creation. One of the great tragedies of our Western culture is that this tradition was, in many ways, exorcised by the Catholic Church. It was there in the Church in the very early days, with the Gnostics and some of their teachings, and it has reappeared for brief moments throughout the history of the West. There was a beautiful expression of it in the Gothic movement in the twelfth, thirteenth and fourteenth centuries, and those of you who have been to the great Gothic cathedrals in Europe, like Chartres, will have seen that the cathedral itself represents the universe in microcosm, and in its sculptures and stained-glass windows are imaged all of the aspects of creation, not just biblical figures and saints but also the cycles of the zodiac, living creatures and plants. And the whole esoteric design behind it is that all of creation is contained within the cathedral's geometric forms, which reflect the divine ordering principle within creation. In the Medieval Era, if you were someone really interested in the depths of spiritual understanding, you could explore that relationship, that understanding of the divine ordering principle within creation as it was expressed in microcosm in the Gothic cathedrals.

And it is significant that Chartres Cathedral, which was the ideal Gothic cathedral—there was an esoteric school at Chartres as many of you know—is actually built on a site sacred to the Black Madonna. Which is, again, the earth spirit—the feminine divine earth spirit that gave birth to this understanding of the mystery of matter, the divine expressing itself within creation.

The Gothic movement lasted for a while, like many spiritual flowerings that come from the soul of the world. But within the patriarchal structure of the Church there was no understanding of the divine feminine—of Sophia—or of the divine principle within creation. One aspect of the Church's patriarchal oppression was to split heaven and earth, to put God in heaven and to see everything on earth as sinful. The earth itself was seen as a dark prison that trapped the soul of man rather than a place of divine expression. And so the *anima mundi* was lost again. But like many true spiritual understandings, it went underground, like a hidden stream, and it reappeared in the Renaissance.

This understanding of the earth as a living spiritual being of course went back to Plato, back to the sacred teachings of Greece and further East. And, as some of you know, there is a tradition that the whole of the Renaissance was started by a master who came from Constantinople on a donkey to northern Italy. There he founded the esoteric school that Michelangelo and Leonardo and others attended. And he brought with him this esoteric knowledge of the divine within creation: of how that works, how She manifests Herself, how She holds the divine proportions. You see it, for example, in Leonardo's Man (his famous drawing of a man uniting a circle and a square), in which heaven and earth are brought together—and in the whole esoteric understanding of that relationship that informs the work of those Renaissance masters.

In the Renaissance, once again the World Soul was understood to animate and form nature according to divine proportions. And once again the garden of the world was enchanted with magical power and transcendent meaning that was implicit in every part of nature, and the wonderful relationship between the imagination and the creative principle in life flourished. It was an extraordinary flowering that really came from the divine feminine within the imagination, and within life, and it was celebrated. Once again the garden of the soul was here in this world. It wasn't just after you died, in heaven, in paradise; it was *here*, in the art that the Renaissance masters created. And this is why, for some of us, the Renaissance touches the soul so deeply now and why there has been a revival of understanding of what happened in the Renaissance. Because it had to do with the divine feminine and the divine feminine within life and that really is an expression of the *anima mundi*. She once again expressed Herself in the West in that beautiful artistic flowering that touches us so much.

But then of course the Church repressed it again, sometimes quite brutally. And the only tradition that was left carrying that understanding, after the tradition of sacred geometry became lost, was the alchemical tradition, which was rediscovered for us in the last century by Carl Jung.[1]

In the alchemical tradition the *anima mundi* is the divine spark in matter. While the Church looked upwards towards heaven, towards the ethereal world, the alchemists looked into matter. And part of their work was to discover how to liberate this spark, how to liberate the light hidden within matter, which is the secret within creation. This divine spark is in every cell of creation. And really, the mystery of turning lead into gold is about revealing what is hidden within the darkness of matter. And so they kept alive, in this underground stream, the principle of the *anima mundi*, the soul of the world. They understood that there is a direct relationship between our individual soul and the soul of the world. In fact, our individual soul is a spark in the *anima mundi*, a spark of light in the soul of the world. It is not just our own individual soul; it is part of the soul of the world. One of the great tragedies is that we forgot this—that, as Jung said, "Man himself has ceased to be the microcosm and his anima is no longer the consubstantial *scintilla* or spark of the *Anima Mundi*, the World Soul."

With the reign of rationalism we have forgotten our place in the world. We have forgotten that our soul, this spark within us, has a direct relationship to the soul of the world. And out of that, I think, came a lot of the impoverishment—soul impoverishment—that we have today. Because once we lose that relationship to the divine within matter, within creation— once we say the divine is only in heaven or can only be found in deep meditation—we've lost something fundamental. And we've lost it for both ourselves and the world.

So humanity became more and more separated, or veiled itself more and more, from the soul of creation. Now as many of you know, if you separate yourself from the light of your own soul your life becomes emptier and darker, more and more meaningless. People would say that is one of the many reasons there is so much addiction in our Western culture: we have lost our connection with anything that truly nourishes us. We get addicted to drugs, or sex, or shopping—whatever it is—because there is nothing that nourishes us. We have lost this relationship to what is present within the soul of creation. We have lost relationship to our own soul and to the soul of creation.

And just to complete this picture, I want to explain something that Jung understood, which has to do with the light of the divine. The light of the divine has two aspects. One is what is traditionally known as the *lumen dei*—the light of God—which is really the divine light of one's higher Self. It is a very, very beautiful light. It is very clear, very simple; it just *is*. It is the light of God as you can see it as a human being. Of course, the *real* light of God you cannot see. You become blinded by it. It is said God has 70,000 veils of light and 70,000 veils of darkness to separate us from experiencing the true light of the divine, which would burn you away. But there is this *lumen dei* that we have within us—our divine light. And when you pray to God your light rises up to God. When you really pray to God there is a light, a spark. You can see it, in a way, from outer space, this spark that rises up to God from the heart of the human being. It is very beautiful. If you go into deep meditation, you discover that divine light within you. It is like a diamond; very clear, very pure, very beautiful.

But that is only half of the way the divine expresses itself. The other aspect is what Jung found in alchemy called the *lumen naturae*—the divine light within nature. One could say that the *lumen dei* is the masculine expression of the divine while the *lumen naturae* is the feminine. It is the light in nature, the light that is present. As a culture we have completely forgotten how to relate to this feminine light. I think for a lot of traditional cultures, ritual—whether dance or song, music, chanting or any sacred act—was a way of being with this light in nature. Through this light you can speak to the soul of an animal, the soul of a mountain, the soul of a tree or plant. It is how you work with the divine within creation. In previous cultures you wouldn't try to live without it. How would you know what to do? How would you know where to hunt? How would you know about the healing properties of herbs? About what is poisonous, what heals what ailments? It was in this communication of light with light—a communion with creation. It was when the world was *alive*. And we have forgotten the world is alive.

I had a beautiful experience the other day, which really moved me somehow. I was trying to understand something and I was taken back in time, to how things were in the early days before this cloud of forgetfulness came. I was walking along a path and I suddenly realized that in those days the path told you where it was going. I had read about the Aboriginal Time when the songlines guided the Aboriginals across the desert. But I never realized that a path could actually speak to you and tell you where it is going. But you can see it echoed in some of the songs of Tolkien.[2] He had access to those ancient memories. He was also a medieval English scholar and knew the stories from those very early times when the path came to meet you and told you beyond what hills it would take you.

And this very different relationship of light to light—our own divine light to the light in matter— is very sacred; it is how we learn how to walk, how to live, in a sacred manner. Because it respects the divine within creation. In the West it has been erased from our collective consciousness. And of course, this country was founded on the terrible tragedy that the Europeans, quite brutally, killed off the people who had this understanding. And those who survived were no longer allowed to speak their native language. So that sacred language was almost erased and together with it went the understanding of how to talk to the magic that is within creation, this relationship of light to light.

In a way, what the alchemists were doing in their crucibles many native cultures did in their daily life—talking to the light in nature. Whether you call it the Great Spirit or the *anima mundi*, it is the same—it is this living divine principle within creation. And I am completely convinced that we cannot solve the problems in the world, the ecological problems for example, without invoking this light, this magic, this wisdom, this knowledge—this *presence* within nature. How can you heal yourself if you treat yourself just as a physical body? Yes, Western medicine does that, and for some things it's good, like healing a broken arm or taking out an appendix, but, as most of us here know, that isn't really the complete answer. We are trying to solve this environmental catastrophe purely on the physical plane, which is missing the whole point. It means we are trying to solve the problem in the same way the problem has been created, which is cutting everything off from its sacred source, cutting everything off from its root.

Fortunately, the transition or transformation that is needed—and I have looked at this very carefully—does not have to happen on the level of mass collective consciousness. My feeling is that the collective consciousness in the West, which is now a *global* West (the whole world has become McDonaldized), is caught in a dream, a nightmare of consumerism. I saw that the energy required to take the whole collective out of that dream would be colossal. There would have to come some mega-disaster, or an enormous influx of grace, or … I don't know what. But traditionally, in the past, changes have always started

just within small groups. They never happened first on the
collective level. Just as, interestingly, when a change happens
within you, when you wake up to something, it is usually just a
little spark within you. A small part of you shifts—ah! Suddenly
there is light. Something changes. Part of our Western spiritual
childishness is that we think when that illumination happens
our whole life is going to change. And we are really disappointed
to wake up and find we still have the same problems with our
partner or job. We don't realize that you have to work with that
light, you have to nurture it; you have to bring that light into
your life. And this takes time, and patience.

If we can just bring back an awareness of Her presence, that
divine being that is the earth, the soul of creation—if we can
just bring Her back, then we create a space where the light
can come back into Her world. It's really just a matter of accepting this mystery within creation. It's not something very
complicated. Just as there is this moment when you allow your
own soul into your life, when you say "yes" to this inner part
of you. This is simply to take that to the next step, to acknowledge that the world is a sacred being. I always find it strange
that somehow we are very keen on working with *ourselves* as
a sacred being but we don't realize that this sacred being that
is ourselves is part of a much bigger sacred being that is the
world, that is creation.

Human beings have a very pivotal role to play. For example,
until human beings welcome them in, certain *devas* and
angels are often not allowed to participate directly in our
life. They are here; sometimes one can see them waiting—
very, very beautiful, very powerful nature *devas*, earth *devas*,
and angels—and they are waiting on the sidelines. They are
waiting while we tear up the world, because they need to be

welcomed in. The earth was given to humanity so we could evolve together, so we could have this relationship between the light of our soul and the light of creation, this alchemical interaction of light upon light. That was what life was always about, for thousands and thousands of years. That's what the mystery of creation was about.

Now when we look at past civilizations like the Egyptians and see the pyramids or other sacred buildings, for example Stonehenge, we don't understand the real meaning behind them. They were being used to bring in that light, to focus that light, to focus those energies so the priests, the initiates, could work with them. So that the lights from above and the lights that come from creation could work together. In Egypt they did it through building the pyramids. In this country they had other ways of working, like the Sun Dance, or for the Hopi the Serpent Dance, ways of weaving together the energies within creation and the energies that are part of a human being. And there are certain very powerful words, given only to initiates, to be spoken only at certain times, that speak to the soul of the world, to the magic in creation. Certain incantations that begin to awaken the energies in the earth—because that's what human beings were about.

The purpose of being human is not going to Wal-Mart and getting more stuff. The whole of life was about making that creative relationship, that spiritual relationship. Yes, there was the concern with survival, there was often famine and sickness, but underneath there was always a relationship to this divine intelligence within creation. But then Western man was given too much power. And rather than working with nature, he decided to control nature. And so he developed technologies to control nature, whether to build a house that was completely insulated or to manufacture chemicals to make the plants grow quicker. We wanted to control nature—which is really the masculine power drive—to control the feminine. And part of that control, from the very beginning, was to deny the sacred within nature. In the same way, the Catholic Church denied the sacred within women—how many women were burned as witches, women who understood healing and plants, who were midwives? You deny the sacred in the feminine and then you can more easily have power over her.

And now we are trying to redeem this ecological crisis with the same tools of oppression, rather than going back to what caused it. That would mean for each of us to take the spark of our own soul and make this relationship again with the spark of the World Soul. It's very simple. Spiritual things are very, very simple.

The World Soul is still alive. If the World Soul had died, or humanity had completely cut itself off from the World Soul, humanity would start to regress, as happens when you are completely cut off from your own soul: you go back to a previous era of your own evolution, to more primitive behavior. You are often drawn back into the destructive aspect of the instinctual world. If we had completely cut off the World Soul, if we had killed Her, then a certain life on this planet would be over. Life might continue on a purely physical level, but a certain magic within creation would be gone; a certain spiritual meaning in life would no longer be accessible to us. You can actually see signs of that already, because for many, many people there is no longer any spiritual meaning in life. They have substituted for that their addictions, or what they can get at the malls. Life is no longer seen as an expression of the divine. If that were to cover everything then the world would be over. It could not regenerate itself, in the same way that a human being cannot regenerate herself without the energy of her soul, without the divine within.

So really, the first step is to acknowledge that the world is a spiritual being, just as you acknowledge for yourself that you are a spiritual being. And the next is to recognize the mysterious relationship between the individual and the world, known traditionally as microcosm and macrocosm, in which every human being is the microcosm of the whole. It is reflected in the Sufi tradition of the perfect man, the *qutb* (the pole). The *qutb* is the one human being alive on the planet at any one time who lives the real potential of what it means to be a human being. And he carries this truth, this potential for the whole of creation. If he weren't here, creation could not rise up to its potential. It's a very important principle in Sufism.[3]

But each of us is in our own way the microcosm of the whole. And what that means is that we each have a direct relationship to the powers within creation. This knowledge has been systematically erased from our consciousness. We read in history about the burning of the books—for example how the library in Alexandria that contained so many of the esoteric traditions of hundreds of years was destroyed, burnt. We hear how the Chinese systematically burnt the libraries of the Tibetans. The Tibetans did extraordinary work having to do with magic, with the powers in creation, and most of their teachings have been lost. There are enormous amounts of esoteric teachings that have been lost. And in the West the Catholic Church got rid of this tradition of the power within creation and how to work with it. The Inquisition did its part in this, and it was very, very systematic.

But there are places where that knowledge is still alive, and you can actually experience it in the land. I have a friend who went to India, to a place near Dharamsala called Tashi Jong, to see a friend of ours who is a nun there, Tenzin Palmo.[4] Tenzin Palmo is a Western woman from England who went to India many years ago and met her teacher there, a Tibetan master. She did the proper training, spent twelve years in a cave, and she is now making a little nunnery in the hills in Tashi Jong, hills where people have been meditating for hundreds of years. And the friend who went to see her there was amazed to find that the hills were alive. She'd never realized what it is to experience the land when it is alive and singing—you can feel the magic in the air when you can feel the *devas* present. For us this is like a myth, an ancient story that happened somewhere else. But there, people have been doing practices that welcome the sacred in the land. They have kept this relationship alive, so the land is alive. The soul of the world is full of all this magic, this creative potential, and it is waiting for us to relate to it, to welcome it back. And we can do this, because we each of us have within us a direct connection to that magic within creation.

The moment of crisis is always a moment of potential. The gates of grace open in a way they were not open before. It is a strange thing: when human beings reach a real crisis, we are given a grace we are not otherwise given. And so it is with the world. There is this grace available now, the energy to awaken the soul of the world before we kill everything, before everything is forgotten, buried so deeply under the Wal-Marts of the world that there is nothing left. When that happens, then the world will die. It's as simple as that. Because it cannot live without its soul.

Or the World Soul could express its dark side, like the *Kali* side of the feminine, and become incredibly destructive. That is a very real possibility. Because as we have forgotten the world is a living being, we have also forgotten the powers of creation can get angry. That forgetting belongs to the masculine myth of domination and control that says we can control nature. We believe that nothing too bad can happen, since, as we're told, nature is not really alive. But this is not so. This is why in ancient times the people were very careful in their relationship to nature and the spirits of nature, why they learned how to talk to nature and to be present within nature, and how to listen to it, how to make a living relationship with it. Now you go out on the freeways and the shopping malls and the TV channels and it isn't there; there isn't even a *memory* of it, let alone any sense of how to bring it alive. So how do we recreate that relationship with the *anima mundi*, the soul of the world, this living presence in creation?

My sense is it has to be done through simple things. Because you always go back to what is simple. It is like what Mother Teresa said: "Small things with great love. It's not what you do but the love you put into the doing." And there *is* a way to perform the simple acts of life, like making a meal, or even just having a bath, with a certain awareness, conscious of being in relationship with what you are actually doing. Remember, it used to be prescribed, although we have forgotten it. Bathing used to be a ritual. Cooking used to be a ritual; the women did it together. They used to sing when they pounded the grain together—they sang the songs of creation as they pounded the grain. It was all part of this very intricate relationship between the energies in creation. But we can't go back; we don't pound the grain anymore. And we've forgotten the chants and the prayers that went with the ritual bath. Nobody is here to teach them to us anymore. They have been lost. And so we have to discover it each for ourselves, in our own way. In those simple acts we do we have to welcome the *anima mundi,* welcome Her soul, welcome Her presence back to us. And then, slowly, we will come back into relationship with Her.

We have to welcome Her in those simple acts first of all because we still have to do them—we still have to eat, to wash, to breathe. Most of us don't have to go into the fields anymore, so we don't sing the songs of planting and harvesting and grinding corn anymore—in the Sixties hippies tried to go back to doing that but it didn't work very well. But there are the *basic* things of life; we can always return to what is basic and simple in life. And time is not the issue; everybody is always very busy these days, I know, but you still brush your teeth. But are you really present in that experience?

So the first step: to give a space. And I think it is easiest to give Her a space, as I say, in those simple, very necessary things that have to do with just being a human being. As Sufis, as in many spiritual paths, we also do it in awareness of breath. If you are really aware of your breath, the breath is extraordinary: with every breath you take, the energy comes down from the soul into creation and then goes back to the soul. If you were really aware of what happens in every cycle of your breath, you would be a liberated human being. With every breath you would come from the plane of the soul, from the clear light beyond this world, and you would bring that energy down into the physical world, into the magic of creation where that light nourishes your own body and communicates with and receives communication back from the cells in your body and the light flowing in your body, and then you would return with that information to the plane of the soul. It's extraordinary.

That's why we do the *dhikr,* or do a *mantra,* with the breath— to awaken that consciousness. It is amazing: with every breath you take, the light of your soul comes down into this plane. And it speaks to this plane and it gathers information from this plane; it has experiences in this plane and it relates to the light in your body. And there is this extraordinary meeting of the light of your own soul and the light within your body. And then it goes back. And if you are really aware, at the end of every in-breath, when the soul goes back to its own plane, there is a moment of bliss. Just for a moment.... It is beautiful. And then with the out-breath it comes back again into creation. So you can make this simple awareness of the breath a spiritual practice, as with each breath your soul, the light of your nature, comes into creation and interacts with this world.

So to make a relationship with God you return to simple things, to what you cannot live without. It's always an interesting spiritual practice to see what you can live without. In the West we tend to accumulate, accumulate, and accumulate. We accumulate things we think are important—and not just things; we also accumulate ideas, thoughts, information. But when you go back to what is basic, you find that life is present. And life is this incredible sacred light, sacred energy, sacred substance. And it is waiting to be infused with the light of human consciousness—this is alchemy. This is the catalytic relationship in alchemy. This is part of the secret that the alchemists understood, the secret of creation: the way that the light of human consciousness is the catalyst for creation. Now, nobody knows what effect this catalyst can have, because we have forgotten about it. We understand what a chemical catalyst can do, yes, but we have forgotten the secret of the alchemists: that this secret belongs to the whole of creation, that creation is also waiting to be catalyzed. It is waiting for this spark to go into it so it can wake up. It's as simple as that. So then creation can wake up. This is the secret of alchemy: releasing the light hidden in nature. Not just the divine light of God in heaven but the *lumen naturae*—the light in nature. This is the presence of God in this world. This is the light of the divine in this world, waiting to come out, waiting to be experienced—because the worst thing would be if it happened and nobody noticed it.

We are here to experience the divine in creation. You cannot know God as pure essence; it would destroy you. No one knows God but God. But you can know God in creation—not in some abstract sense, but in a *lived* relationship to this spark in the world. And although we have forgotten it, this spark *is* the divine intelligence within creation. It is both the Creator and the divine intelligence within creation. That's why in the medieval time, in the Gothic time, they tried to understand the divine ordering principles within creation. They found them in the magic of sacred geometry, the principles of divine proportion. And behind those principles is this spark, the divine spark, the spark within matter. This is the divine energy of creation itself. So, it's very potent, very, very powerful. It can change the world. *We* cannot; we don't know how to do it, we don't know what to do.

I was brought up as a child in the Christian faith. We used to read the Lord's Prayer every day. There is a line in the Lord's Prayer that stays with me now, more and more and more: "Thy will be done on earth as it is in heaven." This affirms that the divine power be present in creation. Yet this was denied when the Catholic Church chose political and worldly power over spiritual power. And now we have forgotten the real meaning of spiritual power. We have even forgotten that spiritual power exists. That's why a couple of years ago I wrote my book, *Spiritual Power*,[5] because I realized we have forgotten it. The Catholic Church brutally repressed it; the Cathars understood it and they were killed—quite ruthlessly. And when the Reformation came, the reformers didn't want to acknowledge it at all either. They allowed that one can work with the individual soul, but they did not acknowledge the soul of creation. They were also frightened of magic. And the soul of creation is where the magic is, where the power is; that is where the potency is.

So, we have a problem now. The world is dying. It is not supposed to be like this. I am convinced that human beings are not meant to sit looking at a flickering screen ten hours a day pressing buttons. Human beings are so extraordinary! They are full of light; they have this divine intelligence. They are meant to live in a sacred way, not spend their life looking at a flickering television or computer screen. That is not what we were created for. And there are powers within creation waiting to be woken up. And we can't take the next step until that happens, just as on a spiritual path you can't take a step really unless certain powers in *you* are woken up. You can't do it.

In the Eastern Orthodox Church some of this knowledge remained—they kept some of the esoteric practices that wake up some of those energies. And of course it is in the *chakra* system in India. It's also in Sufism; the Naqshbandi tradition works with the *latâ'if*—the chambers of the heart—to awaken certain energies. There are esoteric reasons why at some point you need a teacher who can wake up those energies within you—you can't change yourself without them. You can't change

yourself on the level of the mind; you can't even change yourself with good intentions. You need access to these energies.
I always felt that it was really tough that the Catholic Church
decided to make the priests remain celibate—but then never
gave them the practices to transmute their sexuality! It was a
real shame. Because there are basic practices for transmuting
your sexuality. And if you've decided to follow that path of
celibacy you practice them! I have been a monk in a past life
in Tibet, and there, when you were a young monk, you were
given those practices. And my Sheikh, Bhai Sahib, pointed
out that the Hindu *Brahmacharins*—men who practice celibacy
and are given the practices at the right time—have a little
bump on the top of their head where that transmuted energy
has gone to. These practices belong to humanity; they belong
to the magical side of being a human being—they carry the
knowledge of how to work with these energies. You can't do
anything without them. You cannot progress. And that's why
you do a *dhikr*, a *mantra*, why you do breathing exercises. They
are designed to awaken certain energies within you. On our
particular path of Sufism we do a heart meditation that spins
the heart *chakra*. That takes you somewhere else, to a different
level of reality. It's a science—it *works*. It's how a human being
is actually meant to work.

And it is the same for this body, this being, called the earth,
this divine presence that we live in. It is meant to transform.
At this moment in time it is meant to transform. I'm not the
only person who says that. There's a Mayan prophecy that
says that a fundamental change is going to happen in the year
2012—we're going to wake up in a different world.[6] It's the end
of time; it's the beginning of time.

And maybe something is going to happen. There are signs that the world is waiting to transform. Just as there are signs in individuals when they are waiting to transform—they begin to get certain dreams; certain shifts begin to take place—just as there are signs in a caterpillar when it is waiting to enter its cocoon, to become a butterfly. And those signs are visible in the world now. And they're not just in the crises. I personally think that global communication and the Internet[7] are among the signs of the world waiting to transform, waiting to shift into a different level of consciousness.

But real transformation is a very precarious process. When certain energies are woken up in an individual, one can go crazy. When I was twenty-three and my Sheikh woke me up on the plane of the soul, it took me nine months to come back again. It was a very delicate time. That's why when you are really going to transform inside yourself often the energies get drawn inward. Jung used the alchemical term "brooding" for this process. The energy takes you in; you don't have the same energy you had to go out and do things, which is difficult in this very extrovert culture called America. You have to be much more attentive to signs, to how things are.

And that's exactly how it is now in the world. There are signs. And many of us have seen those signs. I wrote about it years ago when I said the magical unicorns that used to be deep in the forest can now be seen on street corners. I experienced it for myself on a very mundane level when a year ago I was driving on the freeway through Berkeley, in the Bay Area, and suddenly I saw a billboard on which was written my favorite Zen *koan* of all time: "The wild geese do not intend to cast their reflection, the water has no mind to receive their image." And there it was on a billboard by the freeway. I mean, what could be more of a sign than that!

But most people are far too busy—this is just the accepted thing today, everybody is far too busy. I don't know what they are busy doing, but they are busy. Yes, life has speeded up, but there is also this American addiction, maybe a product of its Puritan heritage, that you've got to be busy. It's as if Americans are persecuted by time. We have this bizarre, sort of infantile relationship to time; it's very strange.

But there is real opportunity now for those who are actually awake or prepared to be awake, because there are certain things that are going to happen, and if you are awake when they're happening you can take part in them. If you are attentive to the World Soul, She is going to let you work with Her in ways you've never been able to work with Her. She is going to tell you how to help Her to wake up. It's like being invited to participate in a friend's birth. It's really, really amazing.

A few years ago I thought, wouldn't it be great if everyone woke up? Then I realized that was impossible. But *I* want to be here. I actually want to be here *now*—when the world is wanting to wake up, when the soul of the world is wanting us to work with Her. And She is going to tell us what to do because She's been around a lot longer than we have. She'll have to tell us, because all of the books that could help us have been burnt. Yes, there were some books in Tibet—I have a memory of reading them a long time ago. And there were very ancient books in other libraries, but they're gone. You can't find it now in books because it isn't written; it's been got rid of. And the oral traditions of the Native American elders who understood it—they're mostly gone too. But you *can* be there when it happens. I don't know exactly when it's going to happen—there are signs, but we don't know how to read the signs. That's part of the catch-22. Nobody can tell us how to read the signs anymore.

It is such an adventure, to be present with this energy, this power within creation, with the soul of the world. Which is *our* soul—we are part of it. It's not our mother, because if it's our mother we remain children and play the part of children and do not take our full responsibility, or too often become delinquent adolescents. Instead we need to make a mature relationship, what is called co-creation: working directly with the energy of creation, being present. The first thing you have to do is be present. And it's amazing how few people show up even in their own lives. They live other people's lives or how they have been told to live, and they forget they have a life of their own. We have to be present in our own life, the life of our soul and the life of the World Soul.

So you have to show up in your life and you have to show up in the life of the world. And the life of the world is not a shopping mall, or a problem to be solved by economists or scientists, because it's not *made* like that. It is not a computer-generated model. Just as *you're* not a computer-generated model. You're not a statistic. You are a mixture of heaven and earth, an incarnation of a divine spark. And the relationship with the world is a relationship of microcosm to macrocosm, a spark that goes from your consciousness, from your heart, to the heart of the world. It is so simple, so primary, just as everything in spiritual life is primary. It's like that moment in the human incarnation when you become aware of this spark within you, this awakening of your soul. It's an act of grace, a gift from the Higher Self. It's very beautiful how it's done. At a particular moment in your incarnation, the Higher Self is allowed to wake you to your own soul, your divine nature. And after you're given this gift, this infusion of divine energy—you can call it grace—you are no longer the same person. Something in you is woken up. And suddenly your whole life changes. There is this light, there is this hope, there is this sunshine in the eyes—it's incredibly beautiful, the most precious moment. I know when it happened to me when I was sixteen, suddenly the whole world was there—as it had always been, but I had never seen it—full of light, full of beauty.

And all you have to do is to be present and to say "yes." To be present in your life and in the life of the world, the life of the world as it belongs to the soul of the world. We have forgotten about Her for so long. But She is alive. She is here now. And She is waiting to wake up.

*An awareness of global oneness
has begun to constellate. The idea of the unity of
life, that "we are one," no longer belongs just to a spiritual
or ecological fringe; it is becoming part of the mainstream. But
this awareness is lacking an essential ingredient—it is still
an idea, it is not fully alive. When it becomes alive, the
heart of the world will open and we will hear its song,
the song of the oneness of life. The unity of life
is a direct expression of the divine and it is
our lived connection to the divine that gives
us meaning. This song will remind
us of our true nature and
why we are here.*

10

The Light of the Soul

Allâh is the Light of the heavens and the earth.
His light may be compared to a niche wherein is a lamp:
the lamp in a glass. The glass as it were a glittering star:
kindled from a Blessed Tree, an olive that is neither of the East
nor of the West, whose oil would almost shine forth,
though no fire touches it:
Light upon Light!
Allâh guides to His Light whom He will.
QUR'AN 24:35

WORKING WITH THE SOUL OF THE WORLD

Our souls are made of a quality of light, a light that belongs to God and carries a knowing of its source. Through this light the soul sees its way, the path it follows, the destiny that needs to be lived. Without this light there could be no evolution, no meaning to life.

Spiritual life is a means to bring the light of the soul into the world. Spiritual practices give us access to our light and the teachings of the path help us live it in our daily life. The more our light shines in this world, the easier it is to follow a spiritual path and be guided from within. Through this light the inner meaning of the soul comes into our life, and the wonder of God becomes visible. In this light we see the oneness that belongs to God, that is a direct expression of His nature. Without it we only see the reflections of our illusory self, the shadows of the ego.

The world also has a soul. The world is a living being, of which an individual human being is a microcosm. The soul of the world is the spiritual heart of the world, a spinning organism of light and love that exists at its spiritual core. Without this light the world would fade away; it would be just shadowy images without purpose or meaning. The light of our own soul brings meaning to our lives, and turning away from the needs of our soul brings darkness and despair. Similarly, the soul of the world makes the world sacred, and our mistreatment of the world is a desecration.

The light of the soul of the world is everywhere. Just as the soul of the individual is present throughout the body, the soul of the world permeates every cell of creation. Because we can access the soul of the world through our own higher nature, we can access it wherever we are, in any situation. And there are specific ways to work with it, to bring its quality of light into life. There are ways for its light to interact with the darkness of the world and transform the darkness, to reveal hidden qualities within humanity. And there are also ways to help its light flow around the world. When the light of the soul flows around the world, it can open and activate energy centers in the energy structure of the planet, energy centers that are needed for the next level of human evolution, which is also the evolution of our planet.

On one level the light of the soul of the world is the light of humanity, both individually and collectively. It is made up of the light of the souls of all of humanity and a substance that belongs to the very being of the planet. It comes into existence through us and through the physical body of the planet. But it does not belong to the physical dimension. It is fully alive in a different dimension where its light is clearly visible. In this dimension it can interact with other similar bodies of light, other celestial energies that are invisible to us. And the soul of the world is itself part of a vast living organism, a pulsating body of light we call the Milky Way.

In the inner worlds, the light of the soul is guided by the masters of love; in the outer world it needs our attention. The contribution of the mystic is to be open to the inner energy structure of life, to the light of the soul of the world. We can learn to work directly with this light, to become a conscious node in its organic web. Then our higher consciousness can directly participate with the light of the whole—we will no longer be isolated within our individual aspiration, but can make a direct contribution to the way the light moves around the planet.

Every human being can participate in this unfolding. This light is not other than us, and yet it needs to live through us. It comes into life through the core of our being, where we are directly connected to the divine. We need to bring this energy into the outer flow of life, into the places of darkness and the shadows of misunderstanding. Once we step out of the sphere of self-interest into a real concern with the whole, we have access to the energy of the whole. We are open to the light of the world and can use it. Without the light of the soul of the world to guide us, life cannot fulfill its larger purpose; its real destiny cannot unfold.

But there are many forces in the world that deny the world its light. On an individual level the darkness of our own greed or selfishness inhibits the flow of our own light into life. Similarly, our collective darkness covers the world with patterns of greed and desire for power. These are the forces whose stories we read in our newspapers, whose ambitions cause suffering. This darkness is visible all around us. With global news coverage we see how it creates suffering around the world. We see the hungry and destitute and the damage of war. We know the pollution caused by corporations and read stories of their corruption and greed. We recognize how the politics of power care only for more power and wealth, rarely for the well-being of the whole.

What we do not see so clearly is how the light of the soul of the world works, how its energy flows through the hearts of individuals, how it brings hope where there is despair, joy into the midst of suffering. Our eyes are so attuned to the darkness that we miss light's power and beauty. But we can begin to recognize the ways light flows through the world, and learn to work with it. We need to guide the light of the soul of the world into the centers of worldly power. This light needs to show the whole world the way, bring meaning back to the mass of humanity.

Bringing the light of the soul of the world into the collective consciousness of humanity requires perseverance and patience. There are forces of self-interest that resist the light. There are patterns of control that can only exist in the darkness or the shadows, and these do not want the light to affect them. They are often constellated around fears or desires that are based upon illusions. When the illusions are revealed, they lose their control. In the bright light of the divine many forces of darkness lose their power or simply dissolve.

We know how this happens in our own journey: how the light gained through aspiration and given by grace helps us to see the patterns that constrict us, the darkness that binds us. Seeing these patterns with the clear light of consciousness can often cause them to lose their power so that they no longer dominate us. Working with the light of the world can have a similar effect on collective patterns. First one has to break through the resistance to real light—not the reflected light of the ego and the mind, but the pure light of the soul. Then one has to move the light around, so that it can flow with the energy of life, follow the riverbeds of creation. In this way it can nourish the whole of humanity and bring meaning back into the deserts we have created.

Part of the wonder of the energy of the soul is its quality of oneness. In this oneness the energy and the knowledge of how it works are one. In each moment oneness reveals to us how to work with it: how to guide its flow and how to overcome or work around the obstacles that impede it. What is required of the servant is an openness of heart and purity of intention. If we want something for ourself, we cannot have access to the light or learn how to work with it. If we are in service to the whole, we are given what we need to help with the work.

How do we begin this work? In order to work with the light we must accept the darkness, for in His oneness everything is included. We must recognize that darkness—greed, suffering, selfishness—is also a part of our world. The darkness is part of our nature, part of our heritage. We are the fallen angel and this world is our home.

Light and darkness appear to be simple opposites. Like any opposites they can be in conflict with each other or come together in a way that is creative. Our scriptures speak of the battles of light and darkness, good and evil. But our psychology tells a different story, of light hidden in the depths of darkness, and how darkness can be transformed, lead turned into gold.

The time of polarizing light and dark is over. It was a dynamic of the past era of duality. For hundreds of years we have lived within the paradigm of duality, of opposites that are in continual conflict. This was the era of the warring brothers in which the primal forces of life appeared in opposition. So many battles have been fought, so much blood spilled. Another paradigm is now constellating; another era has begun. In this new paradigm the opposites can come together in a new way. We can work with the light of the soul of the world and the darkness of the world in a creative relationship.

BEYOND THE OPPOSITES OF DARKNESS AND LIGHT

How can light and darkness dance together? How can we work with the soul of the world in the density and confusion of everyday life? How can we bring this light into the places of worldly power and help it guide the destiny of nations?

Since the individual is a microcosm of the whole, we can use the model of working with the light of our own soul to understand how to work with the light of the soul of the world.

The light of the soul is not a foreign substance. It is a part of our own nature, but usually remains hidden beneath the coverings of our lower self. Our darkness hides us from our light. But what many don't understand is that the darkness is also needed to engage the light, just as suffering often lifts our face towards God. We may think that our suffering and the divine are opposites, that God is goodness and light while our suffering comes from the darkness. But this duality is essentially an illusion. Suffering is an aspect of life energy being restricted by matter, being caught in its darkness. Often suffering comes from resistance to change, and change is fundamental to life. Even the miracle of birth brings the pain of childbirth. Energy and matter work together; for example, our breath follows the deeper rhythms of life, which is why conscious breathing can lessen our pain and help us go with the flow of life.

There is a flow of life that belongs to the miracle of creation, and the darkness is part of this miracle. Accepting our darkness, accepting the suffering of life, we are taken into the crucible of transformation in which the opposites come together. A deeper oneness is revealed, not as an ideal but as a lived reality. Knowing this oneness, we can participate in life in a new way, no longer thrown between the opposites but recognizing and working with life's deeper patterns, its underlying energy. This is a part of the initiation of the mystic and the shaman, whose journey through suffering gives them access to life's hidden powers. Traditionally such a journey has allowed them to work with the energy of the soul of the world. They know the meaning of the darkness and the purity of light, and how they can come together for individual and collective healing and transformation.

One can only have access to the light of the soul if one lives in the present, accepting what is. At this time in history, this means to accept a certain degree of darkness that is present. One of the reasons that in the West we have so little access to this light is that we are conditioned not to live in the present. We are either chasing our desires or trying to escape our fears. We are rarely content with what is. A Pueblo Indian described this quality of the white man in talking to Carl Jung, "Their eyes have a staring expression; they are always seeking something. What are they seeking? The whites always want something; they are always uneasy and restless."[1]

We are conditioned to pursue an illusive happiness, while being bombarded by the media with images that manipulate us into continual dissatisfaction and desires. The simplicity of living in the present moment has become a spiritual ideal rather than an ordinary reality. If we are to reclaim our heritage of light, we first have to reclaim the present moment. This means to accept the combination of light and darkness as it is. Only then can we work towards a better future.

It may sound contradictory that in order to work for a better future for humanity we have to accept life as it is, but a real future is built upon the present. Only in the present moment can we have access to the energies that can heal and transform us. Living in the past and future, we are caught in our fantasies. In the present we are open to the light of the divine.

In each moment as we watch the breath, we see how energy flows from the inner to the outer, and we consciously participate in this cycle of creation. Being present in our own lives is the doorway to participating in the miracle of divine revelation. The soul of the world needs to be born in every moment, to participate in the constantly changing creation. "God is upon some new task daily." Through simple awareness we connect the higher with the lower, the inner plane of pure awareness with the outer world of events, and our own consciousness with the consciousness of the whole.

When we are fully present in the midst of life, we connect the worlds together, and through this connection the light can flow. We are the gateways for love and light to pour into the world and awaken the world to its own sacredness. Just as *prana*, or life energy, follows thought—which is why simple healing practices use attention and awareness of breath—the light of the soul of the world is guided by our attitude and attention. It follows the orientation of our heart, the way we participate in life from our depths. The more we are oriented towards what is real within ourselves and our own lives, the more easily the Real can flow into the world.

FIGHTING THE FORCES OF FORGETFULNESS

Light is present everywhere, yet hidden and unused. It is covered over by the denseness of our desires and a collective consciousness that has little space for the divine. Working with the light of the soul will open us to a new level of interconnectedness, a knowing of oneness. This knowing is necessary for the evolution of the planet. It contains the knowledge of the future, a knowledge that is based upon oneness rather than duality.

An awareness of global oneness has begun to constellate. The idea of the unity of life, that "we are one," no longer belongs just to a spiritual or ecological fringe; it is becoming part of the mainstream. But this awareness is lacking an essential ingredient—it is still an idea, it is not fully alive. When it becomes alive, the heart of the world will open and we will hear its song, the song of the oneness of life. The unity of life is a direct expression of the divine and it is our lived connection to the divine that gives us meaning. This song will remind us of our true nature and why we are here.

This is like the process of our own awakening. Over many years we might be given glimpses of our true nature, the wisdom and love within us. We work to purify ourselves, to contribute in service to life and love. And one day something comes alive within us. Our heart awakens, and we experience a greater power and knowing beyond ourselves. This is the potential of the moment in the world. Our world's soul can awaken, and all humanity can come to know its true nature.

The world has to awaken from its sleep of forgetfulness—it can no longer afford to forget its divinity. More than any pollution, it is this forgetfulness that is killing the earth. The awakening of the soul of the world can redeem what has been desecrated, heal what has been wounded, purify what has been polluted. Collectively we are dying—we have forgotten our purpose, and a life-form that has forgotten its purpose cannot survive. Its fundamental reason for existence fades away. The awakening of the soul of the world will remind us all why we are here and the whole of life will rejoice.

Forgetfulness is not just an absence of remembrance. The cloud of forgetfulness that covers so much of our world is not just an absence of light. Our forgetfulness of our divine purpose is like a sticky substance that draws life into its web, where it devours any meaning life may have. This cloud is not just the *maya* of illusion but a density that ensures that we remain slaves to our lower nature. Our collective forgetfulness will stop us from hearing the song of the world and deny us our future.

There is much work to be done to prepare the world stage for this awakening; otherwise the dawn will come unnoticed, and once again humanity will have missed an opportunity. We have to bring the light of oneness to the places of forgetfulness. We have to create a network of light within the planes of creation.[2] This network is a container for the awakening of the heart of the world so that the meaning of this event can become known, so that we can hear its song.

But the potency of forgetfulness is such that we have to force open some of the gateways of light. We have to drag the light down into life and fight with the darkness. Once again the battle of light and darkness has to be fought, and once again the darkness has disguised itself in the forms of worldly success. This could be the last real battle at the end of the era of opposites, and much of it is hidden, fought by individuals who dare to lift their faces to the light. Our remembrance of what is real, of the divine that is the essence of life, is countering the forces of forgetfulness and their dynamics of worldly power and corruption. And as always, what happens on the outer stage is a distorted reflection of the real drama of the soul.

When the oneness of life becomes fully alive, it will activate energy centers in life that belong only to oneness, that cannot be accessed through the consciousness of duality. The energy of oneness can link us together; the light of the soul of the world can give us access to these places of inner power that are needed to overturn the entrenched positions of worldly power. This is a work that we are doing individually and together.

There is an urgency to this work, to free the world of certain patterns before the heart of the world opens. And we have to be prepared to fight for what we believe, to commit ourselves to the light of the soul and the awakening of the ways of oneness. This may seem like a spiritual ideal, but anyone who has confronted the darkness of the world knows the intensity and demands of this fight. Unfortunately this work cannot be done just through love and acceptance. Just as there are forces in our own psyche that must be confronted and disarmed before they can be integrated,[3] so are there forces in the world that will not respond to compassion or kindness, but must be confronted with a sword of light.

The potency of spiritual light must be brought into the marketplace of life. In this light we can see things as they really are and so disarm the forces of darkness. The forces of darkness need subterfuge and deception to win us over. Spiritual light will strip them of these coverings and reveal their true nature; we will see how the forces of greed corrupt us, how they deny us our freedom and joy, and how the ideology of consumerism is a plague that sucks the nourishment away from life. But first we have to confront these forces, and although we have to do this individually we cannot do it alone. They are too powerful.

Part of the wonder of the ways of oneness is that we are linked together through our unique individual nature. When we make connections through oneness, we will discover how we support each other in ways that enhance our individual contribution. The ways of oneness give us freedom rather than codependency. And the ways of oneness move faster than the forces of the world. They belong to the next era of our evolution and spin at a higher frequency. If we can connect together through the ways of oneness, the forces of darkness can be stripped of their power. These forces do not need to be destroyed, only disarmed. Then they can be transformed, their darkness integrated into the whole.

CONFRONTING THE COLLECTIVE DARKNESS

Stepping firmly into the darkness of the world, we will confront many of the sins of our fathers, the depths of our collective desecration, pain caused by patriarchal power drives, and the repression and abuse of the feminine. Joy has been stripped from life and our spiritual nature abused and corrupted. Just as our individual journey confronts us with the darkness of our shadow and the pain of our rejected self, this encounter with the collective will force us to acknowledge the anguish caused by our Western culture. And we will have to accept that we are the perpetrators of this suffering. We cannot blame anyone else, neither governments nor corporations. It is our collective shadow we are confronting.

Only when we confront the darkness with honesty and humility can we hope to transform it. Denial and arrogance subtly pull us into their web where we forget what is real. We need to accept our responsibility, to acknowledge that both individually and collectively we have created this dark monster which devours our light. We carry in our blood the sins of the culture we are born into—the people of the United States still carry the violence of the slaughter of the Native Americans. If we do not accept our collective responsibility, our light cannot penetrate the darkness; we cannot fully engage in the fight for our future. Inwardly we remain on the sidelines, spectators rather than full participants.

There are many ways to avoid and escape the darkness, many patterns of denial. But if we are sincere we will be taken to the places in the collective darkness in the inner and outer worlds where it is our duty to work, where our light can be used most effectively. Many mystics now live in the center of worldly life. Faded memories of spiritual seclusion may haunt us, but instead of living in the monastery we may find ourselves on Wall Street; instead of living in *ashrams*, we bring our remembrance to the inner cities. And in our meditation, or during the night when the soul is free from physical restrictions, we are guided to places of darkness where our light can help untangle webs of greed, penetrate clouds of ignorance. Sometimes we awake from a dream half-remembering or dreaming of the denseness, the heaviness that has been around us. One friend dreamed of walking city streets between vast sinkholes full of people caught in unconsciousness and forgetfulness. Another friend was present in a desolate, arid desert she knew to be caused by our culture.

On both the inner and outer planes we can help to create pathways of light where others can follow more easily. We can bring our integrity into the places of deceit and duplicity. We do not realize how these collective forces distort our general perception, how difficult it is to see clearly in this collective darkness. We breathe an air that is polluted and it subtly corrupts and contaminates our natural way of being. And we hardly recognize that this is happening.

It is important to understand that the darkness is waiting to be transformed; its time of oppression is waning. While on the surface the darkness may appear to be strong, its structures of power belong to the past. At the end of any era there are forces that dissolve the passing age. This reflects the underlying laws of creation. In the organic wholeness of life even the darkness follows the cycles of creation and dissolution.

Just as our belief systems appear to be changing, so are the ways the darkness is held. The underpinnings of our whole collective way of life have been removed—which is why we sense a fundamental instability and insecurity. And this affects our collective shadow as well as our conscious relationship to life. In fact it is in the unconscious that changes first happen, as deep archetypal shifts take place.

Living at the end of an era is exhilarating and demanding. The archetypal patterns that give a sense of meaning and stability to life change. This is part of the pattern of evolution. Many people try to hold onto past ideologies and values, while others are drawn into the new currents of life. This creates tension and conflict, and can even evoke repression as those in power try to retain their positions. This too is a natural part of the cycle of change. But the new forces of life cannot be stopped; they are too primal and powerful. Working against them will simply provoke antagonism and unnecessary conflict, and yet this is also part of the process. Some people cannot help but hold onto the past; those most fixed in their ideas have the most to lose.

Working with the energy of the future is dangerous because there is no map. But there is a quality of joy and excitement that belongs to new life. Staying within the confines of the past may give the illusion of security, but it is countered by a growing sense of insecurity easily projected into the fear of terrorism, financial insecurity, or other forces outside of our control. On a physical level our present life is far safer compared with past centuries; we have conquered many diseases and have greater material comfort. But we do not feel any more secure in this safety; rather it appears to constellate greater fear. We sense there are shifts that we cannot understand or control, that the very fabric of life is changing.

This new life needs the darkness; otherwise it will not be whole. In the drama of life there have to be both light and darkness. But we need to work with the darkness in a new way: our collective denial and forgetfulness have created a powerful global monster of greed and abuse. The servants of life are working to change the way the darkness is constellated, so that it too will flow with the new energy of life. Fully confronting the darkness, they are sowing seeds of light in its depths, bringing sparks of remembrance into the centers of forgetfulness. There is a resistance to this work, but one cannot stop the flow of new life. And there are already signs of some of our global financial structures disintegrating, undermined by their own greed.

This is not some minor event, but part of a primal shift in the spiritual and organic structure of the whole of creation.

CONNECTIONS OF LIGHT

At this time of transition the light of the soul of the world has a new vibration; it carries the consciousness of a new era. Certain places on the inner and outer planes where this light used to be directly accessed have been hidden; certain new places are to be revealed. And the work requires a new attitude. It can no longer be performed in seclusion, in places separate from the flow of outer events. The soul of the world can now be most directly accessed in the marketplace of life, where the dense energies of everyday life give a body to its higher frequencies. The light can now be spun into a fine thread that is indestructible and can be woven into the most ordinary clothes.

Because it functions on the frequency of oneness, this thread of light has the capacity to link together people of all different walks of life. And it needs these links to flow more freely. As these connections are made, the light of the soul of the world can flow where it needs to go. The prostitute on the street corner, the doctor in his clinic, the poet with his phrases can all be directly connected, just as the Internet can connect people of all walks of life and all countries. There are no borders or boundaries to the work of this light, and the darkness is also included. To work with this light requires an openness of mind and a freedom from conditioning. We cannot afford to be constricted by past forms or barriers. There is a great joy in this coming together, in being connected through oneness and the light of the world.

In the light of oneness everything is included and life itself will celebrate this coming together, this linking without boundaries. Life is longing to be made whole, to have its essential nature recognized. Through the connections made by this light, life can flow in new ways, and expand our consciousness.

At first individual connections are made, from person to person, from soul to soul, and then these connections come alive and work with their own purpose. We think that a connection is a static line between two points, but a real connection brings a third function. It links the meanings of two individuals to create a new meaning, beyond that of the two individuals, a meaning that belongs to the moment of meeting. This third function has a life of its own beyond that of the two individuals and can relate directly to the whole. This is how something comes alive in a new way, through a meeting that takes us into a new dimension.

One of the limitations of our present understanding of the Internet is that we have not fully realized the new dynamic created by the many new connections that are being made. We do not recognize that it is the connections themselves that are most important, not the information or goods that are exchanged. When these connections come alive, then the Internet will wake to its real potential.

Part of our problem is that the nurturing and meaning of relationships traditionally belong to the feminine, and we have not included this understanding that is natural to women in our technological progress. We are still working primarily within a masculine analytic paradigm, rather than fully integrating the wisdom of the feminine. The feminine kind of knowing has a crucial role to play in the development of this technology.

The soul of the world has the blueprint for the connections that need to be made. These connections are not random, but follow a particular pattern and purpose. In our own lives we know the sudden potency of a meeting that seemed "meant to happen," whether with a teacher, a new love, or an old friend. There can be a shock of recognition, a feeling of wholeness, or the sense that something was given or received.

These connections need to be experienced consciously and with attention; otherwise their purpose will be lost. We must recognize them as important opportunities, even if we don't fully understand them. Some connections will work easily, while others may require persistence. Some individuals who are too identified with a particular mind-set will be resistant to certain connections. But through these connections the light of the soul of the world can flow into new places and awaken individuals to its work. As the pattern of connections grows, it will constellate new patterns for life, for the evolving consciousness of the planet. It is through the connections of individuals and groups that the consciousness of oneness will penetrate our collective consciousness and give form to the future.

This blueprint is not static or preordained, but reflects the organic nature of life. However, certain principles need to be followed, certain energies brought together. For example, over the last few years specific spiritual energies have been connected on the inner planes. This has been part of the creation of the web of light around the world. Some of these inner connections have been brought to the surface, making outer connections. Such connections are a real energetic exchange, a linking of the spiritual energies of specific spiritual traditions. This linking does not dilute the individual nature of each tradition, but creates a node of power that can facilitate further connections.

The transition from an inner to an outer connection is not always easy—in the outer world there are the problems caused by misunderstandings and ego-dynamics that do not exist on the inner planes. As the transition takes place from the inner to the outer, more groups and paths can be connected. Many groups and individuals do not have conscious access to the inner planes and therefore can be connected together only in the outer world. The inner planes and their workings have been hidden from most people in the West; even many spiritual paths do not know how to work directly in the inner planes. So either their consciousness needs to be attuned to this inner connection or the connection can be made solely in the outer.

If spiritual groups or individuals are receptive, it is possible to give them a quality of light that can connect them to the inner web of light. Otherwise a simple human connection can be made. Often this connection needs to be made from person to person. Although e-mail and the telephone offer wonderful means of communication, on the physical plane something can be exchanged from person to person, from heart to heart, that cannot be communicated over distance.

Through these connections the light of the soul of the world awakens a new consciousness in those who are accessible. And this light is the connection—these connections are an aspect of its nature. As the light comes alive in humanity, it awakens the connections that belong to oneness. What is fascinating is how this light has a life of its own, making the connections it needs. There are guardians of the light, and helpers who work with its unfolding. But the light itself knows where it needs to go, the connections it needs to make.

UNDERSTANDING THE FLOW OF LIGHT

Working with the light of the world is an underlying aspect of our shift towards a global awareness. This work is global, and yet it also includes the potential to interact with energies beyond our world. This is a hidden aspect of the next stage of our evolution. Global awareness means taking responsibility for our planet as a single living organism, which then means we will have the capacity to relate to other celestial organisms. Our world is a small part of a vast unfolding whole, each part interacting and affecting the whole. The predicament of our planet is our pressing concern, but as we step out of the image of separation into unity, we will emerge into a very different experience of our world. These changes we are experiencing are far more fundamental and far-reaching than we envision.

Part of this transition is an understanding of how different levels of reality interact. Even to acknowledge the existence of the light of the world is to accept an inner reality beyond our physical senses. Learning how to work with this inner energy, how to participate in its unfolding, will bring together the inner and outer world. We will experience how the light flows from the inner and nourishes the outer before being reflected back into the inner. The symbol of the number eight, with the two circles flowing into each other, is an image for this next stage of human awareness. Understanding the way that the energy flows is essential to our development. Many forms of healing are based upon an understanding of how energy flows in the body. There is less understanding of how the life force originates beyond the physical and comes into the physical plane, although forms of healing and energy-work that work with the etheric body function at the intersection of the physical and non-physical plane.

But the first step is to be open and receptive to this inner light, and to work with the connections that it needs to make within the world. As these connections are made our consciousness will expand—these connections are the pathways of our global consciousness. The connections will open us to a larger understanding and the knowledge that we need in order to function at a global, multidimensional level. Humanity is the consciousness of the planet; we carry this divine gift in our individual and collective awareness. Linking together, we connect centers of awareness within our global brain, and this enables the energy to flow in new ways and a new level of awareness to develop. The Internet is a part of the development of our global awareness, which is why its ability to make connections is so important. It is a web of connections being woven within the fabric of the world, although it does not exist at a solely physical level, but on an energy level we call cyberspace.

The way that the Internet has developed reflects the way that oneness can work exponentially, without being constricted by past patterns of development. It follows the blueprint of the future, which is based upon oneness. In just a few years we have been given a new tool for relating globally and also directly from individual to individual. What is exciting is how it bypasses so many of the restrictions of the past, the power structures and "red tape" that try to control or limit any new development. It is alive in a new way. And this is just the beginning of this new stage of evolution.

We are now being asked to participate in life on different levels: on the interconnected plane of the soul, where we are all one, and on the outer stage where this oneness needs to be brought into our collective consciousness and our everyday life. Without the light of the soul of the world, this work cannot happen—the light carries the knowledge of oneness and the energy of oneness that we need. The light of the soul needs to heal and redeem what has been desecrated, penetrate places of darkness and worldly power. And it has to make many new connections as it helps the world awaken.

It is important to remember that this light is not other than our light. In the patriarchal era we focused on a transcendent God, which limited our direct access to this light. The light of the soul belonged in heaven with God. Now we have to embrace the light and bring it into life. We are the connections that need to be made, the pathways of the future. In our relating we carry the seeds of our collective development, which is why women have such a central role to play. Women understand more fully the importance of relating, how we are all connected together and form part of a whole. They carry these connections in their physical and spiritual bodies in a way that is foreign to men. On a higher level some women are able to magnetize these interconnections with a spiritual energy or substance, which enables the connections that are being made to directly communicate at the level of oneness. This means that when these human connections are made, the individual can awaken more quickly to the consciousness of oneness.

The light of the soul of the world needs the participation of all who are open to this work. But part of our redemption of the feminine is to acknowledge that certain work can only be done by women. The interconnections of life belong to the wisdom of the feminine and a woman's body holds the knowledge of how the worlds interrelate. Masculine consciousness imaged a transcendent divinity—the feminine knows how the divine is present in every cell of creation. Women know this not as abstract knowledge, but part of their instinctual nature—in the womb the light of a soul can come into physical form. Life is standing at the edge of an abyss of forgetfulness waiting for the light of the world to be born. This birth needs the wisdom of the feminine, and women must take their place in this time of great potential.

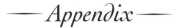

— *Appendix* —

The appendix is comprised of three chapters which explore the role of the feminine on the spiritual quest. The first chapter explores the psychological aspect of the inner feminine or soul figure, her dual aspects of light and dark, and how the inner feminine transforms into the figure of divine wisdom, Sophia. The second chapter describes the feminine side of love, the longing that takes us back to God, and how we need to reclaim an understanding of spiritual receptivity. The third chapter looks at both masculine and feminine qualities needed on the path, and how the sacred knowledge of the feminine and her all-inclusive nature helps us to return to our divine essence.

Appendix I:
The Inner Feminine and Her Dual Nature

Appendix II:
Longing—the Feminine Side of Love

Appendix III:
Two Wings to Fly

---— *Appendix I* ——

The Inner Feminine and Her Dual Nature

Who is she that looketh forth as the morning,
fair as the moon, clear as the sun and
terrible as an army with banners?
THE SONG OF SONGS[1]

THE DIVINE LOVER

The divine lover appears within us and leads us towards union. Within a woman this lover takes the form of her own inner masculine self, her animus. He gives her the power and strength she needs to walk through the burning fire that is the path of love. Within the psyche of a man the same lover appears as a woman, veiled and mysterious. Alluring and fascinating, she beckons him into the beautiful and terrible depths of his own being.

The anima arises like Venus from the waters of the unconscious. She has many forms; she is both virgin and temptress. For many men she is their most powerful archetypal figure, and every romantic poem or song is written in homage to her. From the first time you see her you know that "you have always been her lover." Like Ariadne she holds the thread that can guide a man through the labyrinthine maze of his unconscious, back to the hidden core of his being. She carries the image of a man's soul, of his own inner mystery. It is through union with her that the Christ Child, the Self, is born. In much Sufi poetry the anima echoes the Beloved; in the images of a woman's beauty a divine beauty is mirrored:

> I became love-crazed when my Beloved
> like the new moon, revealed an eyebrow,
> displayed herself, then closed the door.[2]

LA BELLE DAME SANS MERCI

The feminine is both creative and destructive, nurtures life and yet also devours it. The anima has her dark side. She is the siren who lures men into the waters of the psyche and leaves them there to drown. Belonging to the impersonal depths, she is cold and uncaring; she seeks only power and uses all her magical attraction to imprison consciousness. Keats personifies her as "La Belle Dame sans Merci." He describes how a brave knight-at-arms is captivated by her beauty, her long hair and wild eyes, how she sings him "a faery's song" and feeds him "honey wild, and manna dew, And sure in language strange she said—'I love thee true.'" But once she has seduced him, she leaves him; and in a dream he sees all those whom she has enchanted and left desolate:

> I saw pale kings and princes too,
>   Pale warriors, death-pale were they all;
> They cried—"La Belle Dame sans Merci
>   Hath thee in thrall!"
> I saw their starved lips in the gloam,
>   With horrid warning gaped wide,
> And I awoke and found me here,
>   On the cold hill's side.[3]

The same archetypal story is told in the film *The Blue Angel*. Marlene Dietrich plays the anima figure, an actress in a small touring theater which visits a provincial town where the well-respected school teacher watches a performance and becomes entranced by her. He leaves his job and joins the theater company in order to be with her. She totally degrades him, making him act the part of the clown. Finally the theater returns to his home town and she forces him to play the clown before his former pupils and fellow citizens. Unable to endure such humiliation, he goes to his former classroom and hangs himself. As in Keats's poem, the anima has woven her spell, seducing and then destroying her victim.

The *femme fatale* is an inner figure as much as an alluring outer woman, and many men have been caught by her cold passion. They are often unable to relate to women but are fed only by fantasies which leave them starving. One friend who had great difficulty forming a relationship with a woman had a dream in which he was shown the effigy of a witch, under which was written "she can put out any fire." She is the enemy of consciousness and warmth of feeling. Like the spider mother, she is an aspect of the devouring feminine which is merciless and cruel. She alienates those whom she has bitten, leaving them isolated, and, in the words of Keats's poem, "alone and palely loitering."

THE VIRGIN AND THE DRAGON

The power of the anima derives from the archetypal world, for she stands between the personal and the collective unconscious, her image merging back into the Great Mother herself. In her darkest form she is Medusa, whose glance has the power to petrify. Fascinated and yet frightened, man has projected the dark anima onto both the *femme fatale* and the witch. Just before writing this passage I saw a car sticker which read "My ex-wife's car is a broomstick." This "joke" points to the depths of fear a man can have about the dark woman who haunts his dreams, and many innocent women have been tortured and burned as witches because of this fear. Unable to face the darkness within, he has persecuted his projection.

Man's fear of the dark feminine derives from his fear of the Great Mother, the dragon mother, who represents the deepest powers of the unconscious. Hers is a realm in which there is no light of consciousness. In this primal place there is no morality, no division into light or darkness. It is the instinctual jungle world—"red in tooth and claw"—and the domain of the tiger who symbolizes the undifferentiated energy of the Goddess.

This fear of the feminine is very real and should not be dismissed. Towards the end of his life Jung said, "Woman is a very, very strong being, magical. That's why I am afraid of women."[4] If we are to make a creative relationship with the inner feminine we must acknowledge this fear. In myths a virgin, symbol of the anima, is often held captive by a dragon. In previous ages the heroic quest involved slaying the dragon. Man needed to free himself from his instinctual drives and the fearsome power of the Great Mother. Only then could he find the anima, his individual feminine self. While the anima is an archetypal figure, with her roots in the collective unconscious, she also symbolizes a personal relationship to the feminine. A man's anima figure is very personal and intimate, unlike his relationship with the mother in which his individuality is easily lost in the collective nature of the mother archetype.

A man's relationship with the feminine is first held in the grip of the dragon, the Great Mother archetype. A man who remains so imprisoned always looks for a mother figure—for him all women are identified with the mother. In this state there can be no individual creative relationship with the unconscious. In order to realize his own individual relationship to the inner and outer feminine, he must free the virgin, his own pure feminine self.

But in our era, too many dragons have been slain, and we now need the power of the Great Mother to heal ourselves and our world. The anima still needs to be set free, but the dragon needs to be accepted, not killed. We need to look at our fear of the feminine and in the mirror of consciousness see her darkest face. Only then will we cease to project this fear; only then will we integrate rather than reject the powerful energies of the feminine.

The anima often first appears in her idealized form. She is a pure and beautiful virgin. In our Western culture we have separated the light and the dark aspects of the feminine. The heroic ideal honored "Mary, Queen of Heaven" and rejected and repressed her darker, earthier twin. This twin first appeared in the Judeo-Christian tradition as Lilith, the first wife of Adam, who refused to be subservient to him. In killing the dragon we may have freed a virgin but we have rejected the instinctual power of the feminine. The feminine is as much the dragon as the virgin and we can no longer afford to separate the two. We need the primal power of the instinctual world. If we look at the face of the dragon with love and the reflective quality of consciousness, its energy can be integrated. This is a work as much for women as for men, for women need to accept their own primal power as much as men need to integrate this feminine potential. Here lies the heroic quest of our age, for the child of the future needs to ride on the back of the dragon.

In descending into the unconscious, we meet this natural energy of the feminine, which the romantic, idealized image of the anima is unable to contain. We see this idealized image represented in Shakespeare's *Hamlet*, in the prince's initial love for Ophelia. She is "the celestial and my soul's idol, the most beautiful Ophelia"; no earthly images intrude upon his vision. But like the moon, the feminine has a dark side which cannot be ignored forever: "The baying of Hecate is always there, whether it sound from near or from far."[5] Hamlet's destiny forces him to confront the dark side of the feminine in his mother's instinctual sexuality, her adulterous affair with his uncle Claudius. In disgust he accuses her of bestial sexuality:

> Nay, but to live
> In the rank sweat of an enseamed bed,
> Stew'd in corruption, honeying and making love
> Over the nasty sty![6]

Yet what this image evokes is not merely animal squalor, but associations with the Great Mother. In ancient times honey was sacred to the Earth Goddess, and the "nasty sty" relates to the pig which symbolizes the creative female, "the fruitful and receptive womb." Both honey and the pig were associated with the female genitals: there is a Hindu marriage custom of daubing the woman's genitals with honey, and "the most primitive and ancient of the pig associations is with the female genitals, which even in Greek and Latin were called 'pig.'"[7]

Sexuality and fertility belong to the domain of the Great Mother. Here Shakespeare images both her sensuality and her amoral, instinctual nature. Hamlet's Ophelia, his "soul's idol," cannot embrace this deeper and darker anima, and so she dissolves back into the unconscious, first into madness and then drowned in the "glassy stream." Later Hamlet is able to integrate both poles of the feminine, and so realize its transcendent nature. When Ophelia has been buried, Gertrude describes this state of inner peace that follows the "madness" of Hamlet's descent into the unconscious:

> Anon, as patient as the female dove
> When that her golden couplets are disclos'd,
> His silence will sit drooping.[8]

Here the "female dove" corresponds to the feminine spirit of God, the highest form of the feminine.[9] This is the transformation of the feminine archetype, whose dual aspects are recognized as the "golden couplets." In the inner alchemical process the conflict of opposites has become pure gold.

A SEDUCTIVE AND CUNNING LADY

The negative aspect of the anima takes on many forms and she does not always appear projected onto an external figure. The anima is the mediator between the conscious mind and the unconscious and thus through her a man has access to the creative energies of the unconscious. She is his muse but in her negative form she does not allow a man to taste the fruits of his creativity. She would keep his potential trapped in the unconscious or, as in the case of some great artists like van Gogh or Wagner, she so overwhelms him with the creative power of the unconscious that his own individual consciousness is lost in insanity.

Jung experienced this aspect of the feminine as an invisible presence full of deep cunning. When he was working with the fantasies of the unconscious, an inner voice told him it was "art," and he realized that if he believed her

> she might then easily have seduced me into believing that I was a misunderstood artist, and that my so-called artistic nature gave me the right to neglect reality.[10]

The dark side of the anima always tries to lure us away from reality into the fascinating but murky waters of the unconscious. Our defense against her is the power of consciousness, which keeps us grounded in the ordinary, everyday world while at the same time facilitating a bridge into the inner world. Jung stresses the dangers of the anima and the importance of consciously working with the contents of the unconscious:

> The insinuations of the anima, the mouthpiece of the unconscious, can utterly destroy a man. In the final analysis the decisive factor is consciousness, which can understand the manifestations of the unconscious and take up a position towards them.[11]

The anima is a temptress, deceiving a man not only with the bewitching nature of the unconscious, but also with the myriad attractions of the outer world. She is the mistress of illusion; hers is the dance of *maya*. Jung describes *maya* as an aspect of the anima:

> She is the great illusionist, the seductress who draws him [man] into life with her Maya—and not only into life's reasonable and useful aspects, but into its frightful paradoxes and ambivalences where good and evil, success and ruin, hope and despair counterbalance one another. [12]

As Salome she is the temptress, keeping man entranced in the beauty of this world, hiding her real purpose behind a seductive veil. The ascetics who turn their eyes from women and punish their flesh try to escape her power. But only too often this temptress is merely repressed, and she exerts her fascination through the shadow. She becomes a demon who haunts the dreams of the pious.

But once a man has confronted her dark, seductive nature and is no longer in her grip, then the feminine reveals her higher nature as Sophia. Sophia carries the deep wisdom of the soul, and allows us to see through the veils of the illusion and glimpse the real beauty that lies behind. She enables us to see the secret face of creation. Sufi poetry speaks of the beauty of the human form because it is a reflection of the formless. The form of woman holds the highest essence because she is the most beautiful creation of the Great Artist. According to Ibn 'Arabî, "Woman is the highest form of earthly beauty, but earthly beauty is nothing unless it is a manifestation and reflection of the Divine Qualities."[13] Thus, in Sufi poetry, each of her features has symbolic significance representing qualities of the Eternal Beloved. The eye symbolizes the quality of the mystery of God's vision; the mole or beauty spot signifies the Divine Essence itself; the twist or curve of her curl is a metaphor for Divine Mysteries:[14]

By the fragrant breeze from your tresses' ringlet
I am forever drunk;
While the devastating guile of your bewitching eyes
devastates me at every breath.[15]

The eternal beauty seen projected in the wonder of romantic love is a glimpse of our own eternal nature. Sophia draws aside the veils of the dancer, and allows us to wonder at the divine beauty of the feminine side of God. The Beloved for whom we long comes to us in so many guises, and with the wisdom of the feminine we are able to recognize Him in His creation, hear the music that is beneath life's surface, and see the true beauty in everyday life. I was once on an airline flight with my teacher, and looking down the aisle saw a heavily made-up stewardess walk towards me. I have always been prejudiced against women wearing a lot of make-up, particularly when it is an attempt to disguise their natural age. But just as this thought came into my mind, my teacher turned to me, and with the simple wisdom of Sophia awoke me, saying, "Human beings are so beautiful, aren't they? Aren't all human beings so beautiful?"

THE SECRET PLACES OF THE SOUL

Within the psyche the feminine carries the mystery hidden in the dance of creation. As much as she is a temptress, she is also a guide who, like Dante's Beatrice, can lead a man to the secret places of the soul. Once we have accepted her dark face, she can no longer devour us or lead us astray. She shows us the beauty of our inner self, which is none other than her own face unveiled. This is her role in the following dream:

> I am in a castle and am being taken by an extremely beautiful woman to a part of the castle which is not open to the public. It is a secret place which nobody else is allowed to see. I go in. It is a most wonderfully beautiful room with chandeliers. It contains a huge pool, rectangular like a ballroom. In the middle of the pool there are beautiful water lilies in a mandala-shaped flower arrangement.
>
> The pool is full of the most beautiful fish I have ever seen. They are absolutely extraordinary. They have just been fed and I am able to feed them a little bit. They are a beautiful coral color and are big and fat like those very old goldfish one finds in Japan. There is also a frog there.
>
> Then I notice that the pool is also full of giraffes. There is one huge giraffe and lots of baby giraffes. They are able to breathe underwater and are perfectly all right there. That is where they lived.
>
> I accompany the woman and she takes me round the castle.

In the castle of the Self this dreamer's beautiful anima takes him to a secret place which is not open to the public and which "nobody else is allowed to see." Living in the world of the ego and the bustle of our daily lives, we rarely enter the secret places of our own innermost being. Sometimes a dream will open a window through which we can glimpse the wonder that we really are. In the public world our beauty is usually veiled, not only to others but to our self. Only when we withdraw—into the silence of meditation or into the deep peace of sleep—is this veil lifted and we see the mystery and smell the fragrance of our bride, who has long been waiting for our embrace:

> A garden enclosed is my sister my spouse; a spring shut up, a fountain sealed.
> Thy plants are an orchard of pomegranates with pleasant fruits; camphire with spikenard....
> Awake, O north wind; and come, thou south; blow upon my garden, that the spices thereof may flow out. Let my beloved come into his garden and eat his pleasant fruits.[16]

The feminine takes us into her garden, a place rich with the fruits and the flowers of the soul. The longing to find this "secret garden" is deeper than sexual attraction; the garden is filled with the wisdom that belongs to the heart. This is the real meeting place of lovers; in the fleeting moments of sexual bliss we taste its fruit. Sexual ecstasy is a momentary experience of the bliss that lies within the heart, given to us for the sake of procreation. According to Irina Tweedie it is "really the soul and not the body that is the experiencer."[17] If a couple make love with both their souls and their bodies, and in the moment of bliss give everything as an offering to the One True Lover, they can then enter this fragrant garden that is the ecstatic home of the mystic. Mystical states can be very erotic (though the energy is not felt in the sex organs but in the throat *chakra*); in these moments of bliss, the mystic is always the receptive one, the lover impregnated by the spirit of the Beloved. Whether man or woman, we become feminine in this experience; and in its ecstasy we are both enslaved and freed, ravished and purified:

> Take mee to you, imprison mee, for I
> Except you enthrall mee, never shall be free,
> Nor ever chaste, except you ravish mee.[18]

The mysteries of the soul are feminine. In the beautiful room hidden in the castle of the dreamer all the images are feminine. There is a huge pool in the midst of which there are beautiful water lilies. The lily is a flower sacred to the Virgin Goddess, but it also exhibits the quality of the lotus, for it rises from the mud to flower only when it reaches the surface of the water. Thus the lily images the process of inner transformation, which begins in the muddy depths of the unconscious and only flowers when it finally emerges into consciousness. This is why the ego is unaware of the really important inner changes, and the individual so often feels that nothing is happening. The alchemical processes that change our whole being grow silently in the depths, transforming the structure of our psyche from within. Transformations that are not rooted in this way are rarely lasting; they are merely like waves on the surface. Real inner work requires patience and perseverance; only those who are truly committed will continue to walk along the hard and stony path without experiencing obvious results.

But the flowers have opened and the water lilies form a mandala. The beauty of the Self opens before the eyes of the dreamer, and that beauty is always awe-inspiring, for it brings into consciousness our own divine nature. It reminds us of our real home.

> What a wonderful lotus it is, that blooms at the heart of
> the spinning wheel of the universe! Only a few pure souls
> know of its true delight.
> Music is all around it, and there the heart partakes of the
> joy of the Infinite Sea.[19]

The pool is also full of fish, symbolizing the contents of the unconscious which the alchemical process brings together and transforms. But these fish are "the most beautiful fish I had ever seen," for here again the dreamer sees the true beauty of his inner self, hidden in the unconscious. They are "a beautiful coral color." Coral is the tree of the Mother Goddess, and because the inner transformation takes place in the depths, it is under the dominion of the Great Goddess. The Great Mother may resist the evolution of individual consciousness, but the heart is the king and the Self is the master and the "source of every power." Even the Great Goddess follows the will of the Self. Therefore if the seeker—through meditation and aspiration—focuses on this essence that lives within the heart, the energies of the Goddess will help and not hinder the evolution of the soul. Coral is also suggestive of pink which is the color of love. This hints at an inner secret of the path of love: that it infuses the whole psyche of the seeker with the energy of love. The psyche and all of its contents become permeated from within with the transforming energy of love.

In addition to the fish, there is a frog in the pool. The frog is a lunar symbol of renewal and transformation, emphasizing the feminine potential for inner change. But then the dreamer notices that the pool is also "full of giraffes." With its long eyelashes and gentle ways the giraffe is the most graceful and feminine of creatures. These giraffes are happy underwater, for that's where they live. In the unconscious are the beauty and grace of the feminine. These qualities have a deep wisdom, a wisdom of silence rather than speech. The graceful walk of a woman is movement in harmony with nature; for the Sufi the curve of her eyebrow symbolizes the subtlety of Divine beauty. We have become so conditioned to value only knowledge communicated through words that we have forgotten what is contained in the senses: how touch can evoke hidden qualities of feeling, how a caress can convey understanding. The giraffes image the instinctual world of the feminine which has qualities we have long overlooked, but now need in order to bring warmth into the coldness of our rational existence.

THE MESSENGER OF MEANING

The anima can open a man to the music of his soul and thus allow its song to manifest in his life. She is the personification of his creativity, and meeting with her brings its fire flowing from the source of his being. Connecting us with our inner powers, she brings meaning into our everyday world, which each of us manifests in our own unique way. With her hands every act can be an offering of the soul, each gesture creative. Baking bread or writing a song, painting a picture or planting a flower, each can speak of the inner mystery and allow its beauty and meaning to be heard.

Meaning does not come from the external world, but from within, from the archetypal world. The primal, archetypal beings who inhabit it are imprinted with meaning. The archetypes do not have an identifiable meaning; they do not mean something specific in the sense that *bon* in French means "good" in English. They rather have qualities of meaning; they make things meaningful. Huston Smith, the contemporary American philosopher, designates this type of meaning as "existential"; it is "the kind we have in mind when we say that something is meaningful."[20] However, because our language has developed to describe the external world of the senses, it has very few words to describe this type of meaning. We can say that something is "very meaningful" or "quite meaningful," but the different ways in which things feel meaningful cannot be expressed. This is true of our language for feeling as well. In Sanskrit there are ninety-six words to describe love: love for a child is different from love for a brother; a different word expresses a husband's love for his wife from the one that expresses a wife's love for her husband; and the love for a guru is also a different word. In our language there is only one word; the poverty of our feelings is reflected in the poverty of our language. We have not named the different qualities of feeling because we have not valued them. Our rejection of the feminine has caused the qualities of meaning she brings with her to be left out of our lives.

The anima is the messenger of meaning. Embracing the physical and symbolic worlds, she lets us taste the substance of our soul in our day-to-day life. But work with the anima should never be self-indulgent; it should be directed towards a greater understanding of the inner world. This need for a greater understanding was encapsulated in a dream in which the dreamer was about to make love with his anima figure when the teacher appeared at the other end of the room, and, pointing to a symbol on the wall, said to the dreamer, "What does this mean?" The dreamer had to understand the symbolic meaning of his relationship with his anima. This has to be a conscious union, for only then is the meaning of the symbolic inner world infused into the outer world, a place which today has too often become a wasteland.

The highest form of the anima is Sophia, who, personifying the wisdom of the soul, brings the deepest meaning of the Self into our everyday life. In Shakespeare's *King Lear* she is Cordelia, Lear's daughter who refuses to flatter his ego and is banished because of her refusal and her silence. The king then has to confront the dark, power-hungry aspect of the anima in his other daughters, Goneril and Regan. They strip him of his worldly status and leave him destitute on the heath in the storm of his own unconscious. Only then can he find his own inner wisdom, which is so different from that valued by the world. This is the wisdom of the fool, a wisdom well-known to the Sufi. It is the natural wisdom of the Self. When Lear is finally reunited with Cordelia, he no longer cares about the world of the ego, "Who loses and who wins," but looks behind its veil of appearances: he sees his task now as to

> ...take upon's the mystery of things,
> As if we were God's spies.[21]

Sufis are known as "God's spies" for they see into the hearts of people where the real mystery and meaning are hidden. Ibn 'Arabî described Sophia as "an image raising its head from the secrecy of the heart." She connects us with our own divine nature and so allows us to see the inner purpose hidden within everything. Within all of creation is a hidden message reminding us of our real home, for everything—every leaf and stone—sings the song of its creator. Through her ears we can hear this sublime song, through her eyes we can see His face reflected in every sky and every street. Her greatest wisdom is the way that she beckons us into the beyond. In her highest emanation she is the Divine Sophia, the feminine aspect of the Higher Self. Our union with her is a merging into our own mystery:

> Dearly beloved!
> I have called you so often and you have
>   not heard me.
> I have shown myself to you so often and
>   you have not seen me.
> I have made myself fragrance so often, and
>   you have not smelled me,
> Savorous food, and you have not tasted me.
> Why can you not reach me through the
>   object you touch
> Or breathe me through sweet perfumes?
> Why do you not see me? Why do you not
>   hear me?
> Why? Why? Why?
>
> For you my delights surpass all other
>   delights,
> And the pleasure I procure you surpasses
>   all other pleasures.
> For you I am preferable to all other
>   good things,
> I am Beauty, I am Grace.

Love me, love me alone.
Love yourself in me, in me alone.
Attach yourself to me,
No one is more inward than I.
Others love you for their own sakes,
I love you for yourself.
And you, you flee from me.

Dearly beloved!
You cannot treat me fairly,
For if you approach me,
It is because I have approached you.

I am nearer to you than yourself,
Than your soul, than your breath.
Who among creatures
Would treat you as I do?
I am jealous of you over you,
I want you to belong to no other,
Not even to yourself.
Be mine, be for me as you are in me,
Though you are not even aware of it.

Dearly beloved!
Let us go toward Union.
And if we find the road
That leads to separation,
We will destroy separation.
Let us go hand in hand.
Let us enter the presence of Truth.
Let it be our judge
And imprint its seal upon our union
For ever.[22]

Longing—the Feminine Side of Love

The source of my grief and loneliness is deep in my breast.
This is a disease no doctor can cure.
Only union with the Friend can cure it.

RÂBI'A[1]

Longing is the feminine side of love, the receptivity of the soul that is waiting, calling for its Beloved. Longing begins with the pain of separation awakened within the heart. The Beloved knocks on the door of our heart and calls to us to return Home. Then nothing in life seems quite right; something is missing but we do not know what. There is a dull ache in the unconscious that begins to force itself upon our attention. Slowly the outer world loses its attraction, and it begins to dawn upon our consciousness that we want something else, something that does not belong to this world. Then the spiritual search begins. We meditate, aspire, look for a teacher, and as we do so the ache in the heart begins to burn, the longing grow. The more we aspire, the more we blow upon the flames in the heart. The tears that we cry are the homesickness of the soul and these tears point out the path. The pain of love has only one cure: "Only union with the Friend can cure it."

He whom we love is a jealous lover. He will not allow any other comfort than His touch, any other healing than His embrace. A story from the life of the ninth-century Sufi, Dhû'l-Nûn, the Egyptian, illustrates this:

I was wandering in the mountains when I observed a party of afflicted folk gathered together.

"What befell you?" I asked.

"There is a devotee living in a cell here," they answered. "Once every year he comes out and breathes on these people and they are all healed. Then he returns to his cell, and does not emerge again until the following year."

I waited patiently until he came out. I beheld a man pale of cheek, wasted and with sunken eyes. The awe of him caused me to tremble. He looked upon the multitude with compassion. Then he raised his eyes to heaven, and breathed several times upon the afflicted ones. All were healed.

As he was about to retire to his cell, I seized his skirt. "For the love of God," I cried. "You have healed the outward sickness; pray heal the inward sickness."

"Dho'l-Nun," he said, gazing at me, "Take your hand from me. The Friend is watching from the zenith of might and majesty. If He sees you clutching to another than He, He will abandon you to that person, and that person to you, and you will each perish at the other's hand."

So saying, he withdrew into his cell.[2]

A friend had a simple and powerful dream in which she was alone in a landscape crying out at the moon. There was no reply, no answer to the anguish of her calling, and when she awoke she felt a failure. She had called out and there had been no answer. But the tradition of lovers has long known that our calling is the answer, our longing for Him is His longing for us—in the words of al-Hallâj, "I call to you ... No it is You who calls me to Yourself."[3] The longing of the heart is the heart's memory of when we were together with Him. In that memory there is no duality, only union. The lover and the Beloved are one, and so when we feel the pain of separation it is His pain we honor in our hearts.

Our heart calls to Him. We need Him more than we know. Our longing draws us back to our Beloved, and the Sufi has long known that longing is the quickest route towards union. As Rûmî writes: "Don't look for water. Be thirsty." We are poisoned by one sip of divine wine. We become addicted to love. The longing of the heart is the sign of the deepest fulfillment, and yet it terrifies the mind because it does not belong to this world. There is no visible lover, no one to touch or to control. It is a love affair of essence to essence that was born before the beginning of time. The memory of the heart does not belong to time, but to the eternal moment of the Self in which lover and Beloved are united. Caught in the world of time we long to return to our essential nature, to "what we were before we were."

But sadly we have forgotten the potency of this pain; our culture has no place for a desire for what is intangible. In the Christian tradition this relationship of love is embodied in Mary Magdalene's devotion for Christ. After the crucifixion she stood at the empty sepulchre, where he had been buried, weeping. And when Jesus, risen from the dead, came and spoke to her, saying "Woman, why weepest thou? whom seekest thou?" she first mistook him for a gardener until he called her by name, "Mary," and then she "turned herself and said 'Rabboni,' which is to say, Master."[4]

In this meeting there are longing and devotion and the ancient bond between teacher and disciple. It has been often overlooked that Mary Magdalene was the first to see the risen Christ, but it is deeply significant; for it is this inner feminine attitude of the heart, of longing and devotion that she embodies, that opens the lover to the transcendent mystery of love in which suffering and death are the doorway to a higher state of consciousness. The lover waits weeping for the Beloved to reveal His true nature, to be born within her. Rûmî describes this eternal mystery of love's sorrow:

> Sorrow for His sake is a treasure in my heart. My heart is
> light upon light, a beautiful Mary with Jesus in the womb.[5]

Our culture has forgotten and buried the doorway of devotion, and the lover is often left stranded, not ever knowing the real nature and purpose of the longing that tugs at the heart. It is easy to think that this discontent of the soul is a psychological problem and identify it as a mother complex or the result of an unhappy marriage. We need to reclaim the sanctity of sadness and the meaning of the heart's tears. This intense inner longing is the central core of every mystical path, as the anonymous author of the fourteenth-century mystical classic, *The Cloud of Unknowing*, simply states: "Your whole life must be one of longing." The heartsickness of the lover is a longing to return to the source in which everything is embraced in its wholeness. This suffering is the labor pains that awaken us to this higher consciousness, in which love joins this world with the infinite, and the heart embraces life not from the divisive perspective of the ego but from the eternal dimension of the Self. From within the heart the oneness of love becomes life's deepest wonder, for "It is the heart that sees the primordial eternity of every creature."[6]

If we can create a context of longing then those whose hearts are burdened with this quest will come to know the true nature of their pain. They will no longer need to repress it, fearing it as a depression or a psychological problem. We need to be able to collectively affirm this inner secret: that the heart suffers because it has not forgotten its true love.

Longing is the pain of separation and at the same time the affirmation of union. It is the dynamic imprint upon consciousness of the soul's memory of the eternal moment when we are together with God. Each moment of longing reminds us of our real nature, and the more potent this pain is the more this memory is alive within the heart. Thus the work of a mystic is to keep this fire burning within the heart, and through devotion and aspiration to let it burn so strongly that it burns away the veils of separation. Then the memory of union becomes a living reality within the heart of the lover. In the fire and pain of this longing the imprisoning walls of the ego gradually dissolve until the eternal moment of the Self can be lived in full consciousness. The Beloved becomes no longer just a hint hidden within the heart, but a constant Companion and Friend.

Longing is the golden thread of the heart's desire. If we follow this thread it will take us away from the world of the ego and the mind into the eternal dimension of the heart. It is here, in the innermost chamber of the heart that the Beloved reveals His secret face, and shares with His servants the mysteries of love. Those who have given themselves to love's longing step across the threshold from duality into the truth of unity. In love's essence there is only oneness. The lover becomes so lost in love that only the Beloved remains. In the words of love's martyr, al-Hallâj:

> I am He whom I love, and He whom I love is I.
> We are two spirits dwelling in one body,
> If thou seest me, thou seest Him;
> And if thou seest Him, thou seest us both.[7]

— *Appendix III* —
Two Wings to Fly

God turns you from one feeling to another
and teaches by means of opposites,
so that you will have two wings to fly,
not one.
RŪMĪ [1]

THE MASCULINE AND THE FEMININE PATH

Everything that comes into manifestation has a dual aspect, positive and negative, masculine and feminine. Even the primal energy of love has a masculine side, "I love you," and a feminine side, "I am longing for you." The spiritual journey itself also has a masculine and feminine nature. The masculine quality of the path is the turning away from all of the illusions of the world to the Truth, or God, that is found within us. In the past it has often involved ascetic practices, or the seclusion of the hermitage or monastery. Through this spiritual introversion, this journey of turning away from the multiplicity of life, we come to know the unity at the root of all. Finally, completing the circle, we come to experience our Beloved reflected back in creation. We see the oneness in multiplicity.

However, for the feminine the divine is always present. The feminine embraces the deepest secret of creation in which the Creator and His world are eternally united in love. She knows this in the depths of her instinctual nature—it is her natural way of being. For the feminine the circle is always complete because the nature of the feminine is wholeness. The feminine always embraces this oneness because she is made to carry the sacredness of life in her own womb. She is part of the Great Mother who is the oneness of all life. Her work is to bring this deep knowing into consciousness, while freeing herself from life's many attachments.

In today's world there is an added difficulty in that after centuries of patriarchal repression, this instinctual and sacred knowledge of oneness that belongs to the feminine has almost become lost. Many women find it easier to follow goal-oriented masculine values, even in spiritual life. They are drawn towards a transcendent god or the goal of enlightenment rather than valuing their own sacred wholeness. Their deep knowing of the oneness of life and the divine has been buried, almost forgotten. And there is also the fear that if the feminine reconnects with this primal knowing, she will once again be violated by the masculine. She is afraid that the sword of masculine consciousness and its rational nature will cut up and kill life's sacred wholeness.

The work of the feminine is how to reconnect with and live her sacred knowing despite the real fears of it being attacked, desecrated. She has to learn to contain the contradictions of a world in which her instinctual oneness appears lost. Masculine consciousness and our rational world confront the feminine with all the pain of separation from her primal oneness, and yet this consciousness also contains the seed of her development. The rape of Persephone, which for many centuries was a symbol of feminine initiation, separates maiden from mother, but also takes her inside the cycles of nature into the mysteries of the soul.[2]

THE DUAL MOVEMENT OF THE SPIRAL

One of the difficulties confronting the contemporary wayfarer is that most texts describing the spiritual journey have been written by men and emphasize the masculine journey of renunciation. They stress the need to turn away from the world and seek a divinity that can only be found elsewhere. The ancient feminine mysteries embrace life and reveal its secret meaning. But these mysteries were rarely written down and only hinted at in symbolic stories like that of Persephone. In Greece they were taught at Eleusis and for over a thousand years were the center of religious life of antiquity, but it is a testament to their power that despite the thousands of initiates their secrets have never been made known. The feminine is naturally hidden and the secrets of creation do not show themselves easily.

The quality of the masculine is consciousness. While the feminine likes to remain hidden, the masculine seeks to make itself known. The masculine leaves its imprint only too visibly while the feminine is veiled. We live in a culture that values what is visible and easily rejects what is hidden, yet we know we need to embrace both. The masculine and feminine need to be united in our quest, for they are both a part of the spiral path that is our journey Home.

A spiral has both a circular and a linear movement. The masculine is what takes us in a linear direction, towards a goal, which can appear to be upward or downward but in truth is inward. This linear direction demands a focus of intent and a conscious commitment to persevere despite all the difficulties that may be encountered. The feminine is the spiral's circular movement which is inclusive. The feminine requires us to be flexible and continually changing, inwardly responsive to the inner oscillations of the path. To remain fixed is to remain static, caught in a concept or locality. The journey to the divine is a journey of freedom in which all concepts and ideologies are swept away. We need to allow ourself to change beyond recognition, to be swept into a dance that takes us beyond ourself. The Sufi Master Bhai Sahib described where he lived as "a house of drunkards and a house of change."

Both men and women have masculine and feminine qualities and these are reflected in our spiritual drive. In each of us masculine and feminine are emphasized to a differing degree. There is also the collective conditioning that may overshadow our natural tendencies. For some women the masculine focus of the quest is easier than the all-embracing feminine; the ideal of renunciation is easier than the instinctual awareness of life's sacred nature. This masculine emphasis can be the result of cultural conditioning, a wounding of the feminine, or a deep orientation of the soul. Just as there are many variations across the physical spectrum of masculine and feminine, so is a wayfarer's orientation not limited to sexual typecasting. There are men who are in tune with the creative dance of life and can find the Beloved most easily in the mysterious beauty of His forms. An artist may have this spiritual temperament, and through surrendering to his work come closer to Him whom he loves.

In the spiral dance of life and death we need to embrace both masculine and feminine qualities, to breathe in and to breathe out. Yet we also need to acknowledge our own nature, to find our own way of being with God. The Sufi Râbi'a was one of the great women saints and she stressed the supremacy of divine love, in contrast to some of the earlier Sufis who stressed asceticism. Yet she had a quality of inner focus that could not be disturbed. She could not be distracted by the forms of the world, as in the story of when, one glorious spring day, she was sitting inside with the shutters drawn. Her maid came to open them, saying, "Look outside at the beauty the Creator has made." But she refused to step outside, and Rûmî tells one version of her response:

> The gardens and the fruits are in the heart—
> Only the reflection of His kindness is in this water and clay.[3]

Rûmî himself withdrew from the world when he met Shams-i Tabrîz. Divine love called him and he left his family and disciples, making them so jealous that in the end they chased Shams away. With Shams Rûmî traveled the road that leads far beyond the forms of this world:

> I was invisible awhile, I was dwelling with Him.
> I was in the Kingdom of "or nearer," I saw what I have seen.
> ... I have gathered a wealth of roses in the garden of Eternity,
> I am not of water nor fire, I am not of the forward wind,
> I am not of moulded clay: I have mocked them all.

O son, I am not Shams-i Tabrîz, I am the pure Light.
If thou seest me, beware! Tell not anyone what thou hast seen![4]

But Rûmî's capacious nature embraced both the masculine and the feminine. In the same poem he also describes a oneness with life in its differing aspects:

I am the pangs of the jealous, I am the pain of the sick.
I am both cloud and rain: I have rained on the meadows.

Unlike Râbi'a, Rûmî celebrates the beauty and wonder of the creation:

Thanks to the gaze of the sun, the soil became a tulip bed—
To sit at home is now a plague, a plague![5]

To deny the creation is to deny the link of love that runs through all of life. Within the heart there is no separation, no need to turn away from form, because it embraces formlessness. Love is an ocean without limits and the feminine includes everything within her sacred arms.

INCLUSION AND EXCLUSION

Feminine and masculine, inclusion and exclusion—the wayfarer needs both these qualities: the wisdom of union and the wisdom of separation. On the path of love even renunciation is a limitation, as in the saying that "Renunciation of renunciation is renunciation." To be "in the world but not of the world" is to embrace the world with all of its confusions and glory, "the pangs of the jealous, the pain of the sick." When we open our heart to life we are not limited by duality or caught in contradictions. The heart is the home of the Self and the Self contains the opposites within Its essential oneness.

Multiplicity reflects oneness; oneness makes itself known through multiplicity. To deny the wonder of multiplicity is to deny the life that enables us to recognize that God is One. We are not only a mirror to His beauty but a part of His beauty. We carry within ourself the hidden secret of creation, the secret that is brought into existence by the very word of creation, "*Kun!*" ("Be!").

The feminine, caring for all of her children, knows the danger of exclusion. Life is sacred only in its entirety, only because everything is She. True renunciation is not the renunciation of the world but the renunciation of the ego. However, because the ego's identity is so embedded in the outer world, in possessions and attachments, turning away from the world can be a process of breaking the grip of the ego, freeing ourself from its patterns of identity. If our individual identity is contained in an outer position, in a beautiful house or in the car we drive, we are imprisoned in these limitations. Struggling to look only towards Truth, to identify with what is highest within ourself, we need to cut these cords of attachment.

In turning away from the world, the wayfarer is turning from the ego towards the Self. The Self, "lesser than the least, greater than the greatest," is a quality of wholeness that contains everything, including all life, within Itself. The Self cannot exclude anything, as reflected in the story of the soldier who asked the Sufi master Jâmî if he was a thief. The great saint replied, "What am I not?" Turning towards the Self, the wayfarer's personal self becomes included within the greater dimension of his innermost being: "whole, he passes into the Whole."[6]

Renunciation is a falling away of attachments as the wayfarer is caught and held within the larger dimension of the Self. The lesser falls away under the influence of the greater. Each step we take on the path towards Truth increases the influence of the Self, whose energy has the effect of dissolving patterns of ego attachments. The Self gives the wayfarer the power to turn away from the world. Without this power we would be forever under the spell of the ego and its patterns of illusion. The ego is so strong and its attachments so potent that the wayfarer could never break its grip. Only because we are included within the gravitational pull of the Self are we able to make the transition, step into the spiral of the path.

At the root of renunciation is the Self's totality of inclusion. But this inclusion demands that we leave behind the ego, that we "die before we die." We need to cooperate with the energy of wholeness that separates us from our own identity, our values and attachments. We need to see the limitations of our own life as we know it, its emptiness and illusory nature. To be embraced by the Self is to have to break through the barriers the ego has created to protect itself. We need the sword of love to cut us away from our attachments, just as we need the warmth of love to melt the boundaries of our own existence.

Contraction and expansion, in-breathing and out-breathing, the path is a continual process of movement and change. There are times when we need to focus and keep our attention one-pointed. But there are also periods of expansion when the heart opens to include a diversity of experiences, when the manifold aspects of both ourself and the Beloved come into consciousness. The real limitation is to remain caught in one stage, in the masculine dynamic of contraction or the feminine quality of expansion. Each has its time and purpose, and then changes into its opposite. The guidance of the Self and the energy of the path activate the movement of the spiral and the inner process that accompanies it. The danger is that we can remain attached to a particular spiritual dynamic. For each of us, different aspects of the path are easier and more appealing. Some wayfarers find the masculine energy of renunciation more attractive, while the feminine work of inclusion may evoke feelings of vulnerability. Others are naturally attuned to the work of embracing, and find the knife of real discrimination and detachment difficult to wield.

DIFFERENT CHALLENGES FOR MEN AND WOMEN

We all have both masculine and feminine qualities within us, but men and women are made differently: physically, psychologically, and spiritually. Because a woman creates new life from her own body she has an instinctual understanding of the spiritual essence of life. This knowledge comes from the creative power of God which she receives in her spiritual and psychic centers at birth. A man has to work hard to gain this knowledge. A man needs to transmute his instinctual power drive until it is surrendered to the will of God. A woman's instinctual nature always connects her with the spiritual essence of life, but man's instinctual drive has to be transformed in order to realize its divine potential. In her natural self, woman is always at the sacred center. A man has to make his heroic journey in order to rediscover within himself his spiritual nature.

Women instinctively know life's wholeness, but find it difficult to leave outer attachments. Generally it is easier for men to be detached and to focus on an invisible goal. Irina Tweedie explains this:

> Because women have children they are made in such a way that things of this world are more important than for a man. We need warmth, we need security. For a woman a home, warmth, security, love, are very much more important than for a man. You will see in India many more male *sannyasins* than female *sannyasins*. For a woman it is much more difficult to renounce the world…. For us women spiritual life is easier than for men, but to renounce is more difficult than for men.[7]

For a woman, detachment can carry the pain of cutting her away from the all-inclusive nature of life. Although the Great Mother embraces everything, in one of her aspects she requires that her children remain unconscious and bound to her in servitude. The spiritual path takes us beyond the limits of created nature: we become bound to the Creator and not to creation. The wayfarer bows down before no one but God. Detachment is the work of freeing oneself from the grip of creation's many attachments while at the same time honoring its sacred nature.

The alchemists called the process of transformation an *opus contra naturam* because they understood how the enclosed cycle of nature must be broken for a higher level of consciousness to evolve. Consciousness involves separation, and while the feminine honors the wholeness of life she also needs to break free from a total dependence upon the Great Mother. The symbol of *ouroboros*, the serpent eating its tail, images the realm of the Great Mother in which everything returns upon itself, and the wheel of life keeps us endlessly imprisoned.

A boy's passage into manhood instinctually frees him from the mother. His spiritual journey is then to rediscover this sacred wholeness within himself. The girl never leaves the arms of the Great Mother, and womanhood is a celebration of her belonging to the creative cycle. A girl's first menstruation symbolizes how she holds the power of creation within her body and can herself become a mother. Learning to become detached can feel like a violation of life's all-embracing nature, and can also carry the guilt that comes with freedom and higher consciousness.

Guilt is a weapon that the Great Mother wields with great effectiveness in order to keep her children imprisoned. Women, being closer to the Great Mother, are more susceptible to the effects of guilt. For example, a woman who was on retreat became aware that although she loved her husband and children, she was also quite happy alone. This revelation surprised her with a new-found inner freedom, but she quickly felt guilty: "Maybe it is wrong to feel happy being alone when I am a mother and wife." Through such feelings of guilt the Great Mother works to draw her daughter back into the womb of the collective where she belongs just as mother and wife. The woman at the retreat needed to be reassured of the importance of the new consciousness awakening within her, and that it was in no way contradictory to her maternal role.

The spiritual journey is a work of bringing into consciousness our own inner connection to the Beloved. Every soul carries the imprint of His face, the memory of His nearness. Bringing the heart's remembrance into daily life means to consciously acknowledge our spiritual dimension. While women are more instinctively attuned to the sacred, consciousness is a masculine quality. The nature of the feminine is to remain hidden and veiled, and the Great Mother has placed a great taboo upon consciousness. To make conscious the mystery of life's sacred essence can feel like a violation of Her command to keep this secret hidden.

Consciousness also carries the pain of limitation. The nature of the unconscious is unlimited and undefined. The ocean of the unconscious is without borders or differentiation. The moment something is made conscious it is defined and limited by this definition. To say something is "like this" excludes it from being otherwise. This is against the all-inclusive nature of the feminine. The feminine also knows the danger of definition, how easily life can become crystallized and lose its dynamic, evolutionary nature. The essence of life cannot be fixed or limited, and in the very process of naming what is sacred its eternal nature can be lost. The ancient wisdom of the Tao expresses this:

> The tao that can be told
> is not the eternal Tao.
> The name that can be named
> is not the Eternal name.
> The unnameable is the eternally real.
> Naming is the origin
> of all particular things.
>
> Free from desire, you realize the mystery.
> Caught in desire, you see only the manifestations.
>
> Yet mystery and manifestations
> arise from the same source.
> This source is called darkness.
>
> Darkness within darkness.
> The gateway to all understanding.[8]

The feminine knows the mystery and instinctually feels the peril of making this mystery conscious. What the heart knows cannot be understood with the mind. Yet the spiritual path involves the work of bringing together the inner and outer worlds, living outwardly in harmony with one's innermost self. Keeping one's feet upon a path which is "as narrow as the edge of a razor" needs the light of conscious discrimination. We need to see the path as clearly as we are able. Ultimately the wayfarer knows that he cannot know, as in the prayer of Abû Bakr: "Praise to God who hath given His creatures no way of attaining to the knowledge of Him except through their inability to know Him."[9] But in order to live in this world as His servant, constantly attentive to His will, we need to know in the mind as well as in the heart that we belong to Him.

The feminine, attuned to the mystery of what is hidden, can experience consciousness as a cruel and bleak light that brings limitation and misunderstanding. The sacred can seem violated by a harshness that denies both subtlety and change. There is a further difficulty in that the consciousness of our contemporary world is dominated by rationalism and materialism. As a result we lack even the language to describe the qualities of the soul. Our language has developed to describe a rational view of a tangible outer reality, and the poverty of language to articulate feelings is an example of our difficulty in describing a fluid, irrational, inner experience. The inner world and its experiences lack the clear divisions that characterize the outer world. A similar limitation of verbal language has become evident in describing recent sub-atomic field theories, where

> ...the task of articulation requires that a vision of a dynamic, mutually interacting field be represented through a medium that is inherently linear, fragmented and unidirectional.[10]

Bringing consciousness to the soul confronts the wayfarer with a collective culture, its language and thought-forms, that have for centuries rejected the sacred in favor of the rational and the material. The limitations of consciousness have never been more evident.

One further difficulty confronting women in our Western culture is the way its masculine values in themselves can be experienced as a violation of the feminine. Entering the patriarchal workplace, women are often forced to adopt masculine attitudes and goals that violate their instinctual awareness of the sacred wholeness of life. In order to compete or just survive in today's world a woman may have had to sacrifice her nurturing, maternal self. The emptiness that many people feel in today's material culture can be traced to the fact that the feminine's role of carrying the sacred meaning of life has been rejected and forgotten. The quality of joy that belongs to life lived from a sacred center has been replaced by a search for pleasure. We all suffer from this collective impoverishment, but women, being closer to the core of creation, feel this desolation and violation more strongly. Yet for the same reason more women than men are at the present time attracted to spiritual life. Women feel more acutely the need within themselves and within the collective to remedy this primal pain. But at the same time there is an understandable fear that the mystery which they bring from the soul into consciousness will be again abused and rejected.

A man needs to rediscover what has been lost to masculine consciousness, learn to surrender his instinctual power drive so that the feminine soul can give birth to the divine mystery. He has to cross the threshold of vulnerability and lay down his sword at the feet of his inner feminine. A woman carries the divine essence in every cell of her body, in the very substance of herself. She needs to bring this sacred self into consciousness despite the fear of violation and pain of misunderstanding. Freeing herself from her attachments in this world, she is able to consciously know and nourish others with the mystery that forms the fabric of her being:

> Free from desire, you realize the mystery.
> Caught in desire, you see only the manifestations.

THE CIRCLE OF THE SELF

While the arms of the Great Mother embrace all of creation, the circle of the Self includes the two worlds. Real renunciation is not a denial of life but an affirmation of the soul's freedom. Consciously acknowledging our spiritual nature, we step off the endless cycle of life and death onto the spiral path that leads to the very center, traditionally the mystical marriage of masculine and feminine. From this marriage the divine child of our true nature is born, our divine consciousness that sees things as they really are.

The wayfarer's conscious commitment to his or her spiritual self is the key that opens the door to this path beyond the illusions of creation. Locked within the ego we see only the attachments of this world. When we affirm the Self we begin the work of limiting the ego's autonomy. This work of limitation is a period of constriction that is painful and demanding. But it is mirrored by an inner expansion as the dimension of the Self opens within us. This inner expansion is not immediately accessible to consciousness. But gradually, hidden from our own perception, a new organ of consciousness is born. The eye of the heart begins to open.

We need perseverance if we are to stay on the path as the experience of limitation intensifies. We need to remain true to our heart's deepest desire despite the difficulties placed in our way by the dying ego. As the ego's horizon closes in we have to trust that we are being guided and not deceived. This period of transition usually lasts for several years, although it will vary in intensity. The opening of the eye of the heart takes time and requires patience.

Gradually we make the transition from the ego to the Self. When the ego is surrendered, we step into the all-embracing realm of the Self. The Self allows the ego the autonomy it needs in order to function in everyday life. But the wayfarer needs to keep constant vigilance as the ego may try to overstep its boundaries and increase its power. We need to keep an inner eye always watching that the ego not make new attachments, that we remain free. Constantly

The Return of the Feminine and the World Soul

vigilant, we know that the ego waits behind every corner, subtly trying to seduce us back into the illusions of the world. Sometimes the ego can become frightened by a deepening awareness of the infinite inner space, of a love that has no attachments, and try to pull us back from this brink. But once we are surrendered we are protected and guided by the energy of the Self. Spiritual evolution does not go backwards.

NO BIRD AND NO WING

Surrendered to the Self, the wayfarer is in a state of both total inclusion and total renunciation. Everything within the two worlds is held within the circle of the Self, a circle "whose center is everywhere and circumference nowhere." The Self is free from any limitation, any attachment. Free even from the need for renunciation, the lover looks only to the Beloved. This is the state of mystical poverty, the poverty of the heart, whose "inner truth is that the servant is independent of all except God."[11] Mystical poverty is the heart's inner attachment to its Beloved and freedom from all other attachments. It is in this sense that the Sufi regards absolute poverty as absolute richness.

Mystical poverty allows the lover to know the Beloved in the inner and outer worlds. Attached to the world of forms, we see only the outer shape of creation. Unattached to forms, the eye of the heart sees the secret hidden in the outer world, the feminine mystery of creation that came into being with the command "*Kun!*". In the words of 'Attâr:

> If the eye of the heart is open
> In each atom there will be one hundred secrets.[12]

The Sufi poet Shûshtarî describes how the state of poverty draws the lover into the inner mystery of her own being, where she is able to make the true connection between the outer and inner world, and thus realize creation's secret:

> If my clay veils me
> from my essence,
> the richness of my poverty
> draws me to me.
> You who seek poverty,
> if you connect
> the corporeal world
> with the Secret,
> creation and its mandate,
> the Name will be revealed to you at once.
> You will see the extent
> of the command—kun!—
> and He Who is its Initiator.[13]

Poverty is an inner emptiness which reveals the Name hidden at the core of creation. Within the heart, poverty is a state of surrender in which there is only the oneness of love. Love's oneness is symbolized by the first letter of the Arabic alphabet, ﺍ (*Alif*), which "represents graphically the straightness, non-deviation and unity of all opposites within the source and beginning of phenomena."[14] This oneness which is both the beginning and the end of creation is eternally present within every atom. For the lover this one letter, *Alif*, is written in fire on the back of the heart. Within the heart God's oneness burns away the veils of duality. Externally the lover may remain in the world of multiplicity, but his love for God has merged into God's love for him. Najm al-Dîn Kubrâ explains this state in which the opposites have been united and then dissolved:

> When the lover is annihilated in Love his love becomes one with the Love of the Beloved, and then there is no bird and no wing, and his flight and love to God are by God's Love to him, and not to Him by him.[15]

As we travel the path of love, the opposites spiral inward towards the center where the two worlds meet. What we know as ourselves, the form of the lover, remains in the outer world of opposites. We feel the fluctuations of the heart, the expansions and contractions of love. But inwardly the states of the lover, the stages of the journey, have been replaced by the effects of the Beloved, "who holds the heart of the faithful between two of His fingers and turns it as He wills." The masculine and feminine aspects of the path are merged into oneness as "The mystic passes away from what belongs to himself and persists through what belongs to God, while conversely he persists through what belongs to God, and so passes away from what belongs to himself...."[16]

Notes

1. Quoted by Chittick, *Imaginal Worlds*, p. 80.

1. RECLAIMING THE FEMININE MYSTERY OF CREATION

1. Trans. by Barbara Newman, *Sister of Wisdom: St. Hildegard's Theology of the Feminine*, p 63.
2. See the writings of Helen Luke, in particular *Woman: Earth and Spirit*, p. 3.

2. THE CONTRIBUTION OF THE FEMININE

1. *"Kun!"* ("Be!") is an Arabic word referring to the act of manifesting, existing, or being. In the Qur'an, Allâh commands the universe to be (*"kun!"*), and it is (*fayakun*).
2. Sufism is a path of love in which God, or Truth, is experienced as the Beloved. See Vaughan-Lee, *Sufism: the Transformation of the Heart*, p. 1.

3. PATRIARCHAL DEITIES AND THE REPRESSION OF THE FEMININE

1. Bedagi, a member of the Wabankis Nation, quoted by T. C. McLuhan, *Touch the Earth*, p. 22.
2. Because of the nature of these experiences, some mystics (for example Ibn 'Arabî) are often mistakenly labeled pantheists.
3. For more on the story of Yusuf (Joseph) and Zulaikha, see Vaughan-Lee, *Catching the Thread*, pp. 157-168, or *Yusuf and Zulaikha* by Jâmî.

4. FEMININE CONSCIOUSNESS AND THE MASCULINE MIND

1. To listen to this talk, which is part of the audio series, "Exploration of Darkness and the Misuse of Magic," recorded in Germany in 2006, visit The Golden Sufi Center online audio archive library: www. goldensufi.org/audioarchives.html.
2. For further information, see "Exploration of Darkness and the Misuse of Magic" by Llewellyn Vaughan-Lee, recorded in Germany in 2006. This series of talks explores different dimensions of darkness, explaining how dark magic began with the misuse of the natural magic of creation. Through this misuse the natural harmony of life was distorted, and doorways to darkness were opened. If we are to restore the natural

balance, we need to return to this misuse and undo its dark magic with the greater power of love.
3. Bhai Sahib was the Sufi Sheikh of Irina Tweedie. See Irina Tweedie, *Daughter of Fire: A Diary of a Spiritual Training with a Sufi Master,* pp. 634-635.

5. THE SACRED FEMININE AND GLOBAL TRANSFORMATION

1. See *Appendix II: Longing—the Feminine Side of Love,* pp. 191-195.
2. See Vaughan-Lee, *Alchemy of Light,* ch. 4, "Images of Life," pp. 53-69.
3. C. G. Jung, *Collected Works,* vol. 18, "The Tavistock Lectures," p. 163.
4. For further information on the Internet as a living symbol, see *Alchemy of Light,* pp. 61-62 and pp. 133-134; *Working with Oneness,* p. 11; and www.workingwithoneness.org/internet.html
5. *Alchemy of Light,* ch. 4, "Images of Life."
6. For further information on the emerging global consciousness of oneness, see www.workingwithoneness.org.

6. WOMEN AND HEALING THE EARTH

1. To listen to this talk, visit The Golden Sufi Center audio archive library: www. goldensufi.org/audioarchives.html.

7. THE ENERGY OF MATTER

1. *The Book of Secrets,* trans. from the French by Lynn Finegan.
2. See Vaughan-Lee, *Awakening the World: A Global Dimension to Spiritual Practice,* The Golden Sufi Center, 2006.
3. William Chittick, *The Sufi Path of Knowledge,* pp. 154–155.
4. *Tao Te Ching,* trans. Gia-Fu Feng and Jane English, Fifty-Nine.
5. Heisenberg's Uncertainty Principle, "The more precisely the position is known, the less precisely the momentum is known," points to this dynamic.
6. See Vaughan-Lee, *Working with Oneness,* ch. 7, "Magic."
7. Martin Prechtel, "Saving the Indigenous Soul," *The Sun,* April 2001.
8. See the work of Peter Kingsley on Parmenides, Empedocles, and the origins of Western civilization: www.peterkingsley.org.
9. Rûmî, trans. Andrew Harvey, *The Mystic Vision,* p. 144.
10. Shabistarî, *The Secret Rose Garden,* trans. Florence Lederer, p. 85.

8. ANIMA MUNDI: AWAKENING THE SOUL OF THE WORLD

1. Stephan Hoeller, *Gnosis: A Journal of Western Inner Traditions*, vol. 8, Summer 1988.
2. Timaeus 30D3-31A1, *Plato's Timaeus*, trans. F. M. Cornfield.
3. There is a tradition that medieval stained-glass makers were taught by alchemists how to use glass to transform light.
4. David Fideler, *The Soul of the Cosmos*, p.138. Richard Tarnas, *The Passion of the Western Mind*, p. 213.
5. Giordano Bruno, *Cause, Principle, and Unity*, trans. Jack Lindsay, p. 81.
6. Alchemical text quoted by C. G. Jung, *Collected Works*, vol. 8, para. 388.
7. C. G. Jung, *Collected Works*, vol. 14, para. 372.
8. See John Eberly, *Al-Kimia: The Mystical Islamic Essence of the Sacred Art of Alchemy*.
9. The Hermetic Museum, 1:13, quoted by Edward Edinger in *Anatomy of the Psyche*, p. 11. See also Vaughan-Lee, *Catching the Thread*, p. 66ff.
10. Quoted by Edinger, *Anatomy of the Psyche*, p. 231. Hermes Trismegistos is the "patron" of the alchemical art. According to legend, the original Emerald Tablet was found in the tomb of Hermes Trismegistos by Alexander the Great. "It is the cryptic epitome of the alchemical *opus*, a recipe for the second creation of the world, the *unus mundus*."
11. *Poems and Prose of Gerard Manley Hopkins*, "God's Grandeur."
12. Ghalib, trans. Jane Hirshfield, *The Enlightened Heart*, ed. Stephen Mitchell, p. 105.
13. *Collected Works*, vol. 11, p. 759
14. David Fideler, *The Soul of the Cosmos*, p. 100.
15. http://en.wikipedia.org/wiki/The_Garden_of_Cyrus
16. Paul Oskar Kristeller, *The Philosophy of Marsilio Ficino*, p. 120.
17. Hermes Trismegistos, *The Emerald Tablet*, 4 & 5.
18. "Therefore you should carefully test and examine the life, character, and mental aptitude of any person who would be initiated in this Art." The Hermetic Museum, 2:12, quoted by Edward Edinger, *Anatomy of the Psyche*, p. 7.
19. E. E. Cummings, *Selected Poems 1923-1958*, "i thank You God for most this amazing."

9. INVOKING THE WORLD SOUL

1. See C. G. Jung, *Collected Works*, vol. 12, "Alchemical Studies" and vol. 14, "Mysterium Coniunctionis."
2. See the writings of J. R. R. Tolkien, including *The Hobbit* and *The Lord of the Rings* trilogy.

3. See Vaughan-Lee, *Working with Oneness*, pp. 4-5.
4. See Tenzin Palmo's website for information on the Tibetan nunnery, Dongyu Gatsal Ling, and her work: www.tenzinpalmo.com. Also see Vicki Mackenzie's biography, *Cave in the Snow: Tenzin Palmo's Quest for Enlightenment*, and the DVD, *Cave in the Snow*, directed by Liz Thompson.
5. See Vaughan-Lee, *Spiritual Power: How It Works*.
6. See *The Mystery of 2012: Predictions, Prophecies, and Possibilities*, from Sounds True.
7. See *Alchemy of Light*, pp. 61-62 and pp. 133-134; *Working with Oneness*, p. 11; and www.workingwithoneness.org/internet.html

10. THE LIGHT OF THE SOUL

1. C. G. Jung, *Memories, Dreams, Reflections*, p. 276.
2. See *Alchemy of Light*, ch. 2, "The Light of the World," also pp. 68-69.
3. In Islam this fight against the *nafs* or "lower nature" is called the *Greater Jihad*. The fight against the unbeliever is the *Lesser Jihad*.

APPENDIX I: THE INNER FEMININE AND HER DUAL NATURE

1. *Song of Songs*, 6:10.
2. Hâfiz, in Javad Nurbakhsh, *Sufi Symbolism*, vol. 1, p. 6.
3. Keats, "La Belle Dame sans Merci," x-xi.
4. Recorded by Suzanne Percheron, in *C. G. Jung, Emma Jung and Toni Wolff: A Collection of Remembrances*, p. 53.
5. Jung, *Collected Works*, vol. 14, para. 216.
6. Shakespeare, *Hamlet*, III.iv. 91-94.
7. Erich Neumann, *The Origins and History of Consciousness*, p. 85.
8. *Hamlet*, V.i. 281-283.
9. In *The Acts of Thomas* there is a Eucharistic prayer which uses similar imagery to worship the Holy Ghost in its feminine form:
   Come holy dove,
   Which hast brought forth the twin nestlings;
   Come secret mother...
   quoted by Jung, *Collected Works*, vol. 5, para. 561.
10. Jung, *Memories, Dreams, Reflections*, p. 212.
11. ibid., p. 212.
12. Jung, *Collected Works*, vol. 9ii, para. 24.
13. Quoted by Laleh Bakhtiar in *Sufi Expressions of the Mystic Quest*, p. 21.
14. See Javad Nurbakhsh, *Sufi Symbolism*, vol. 1.
15. Hâfiz, in *Sufi Symbolism*, vol. 1, p. 23.

16. *Song of Songs*, 4:12-16.
17. Irina Tweedie, quoted by Roger Housden in *The Fire in the Heart*, p. 164.
18. John Donne, "Batter my Heart, three person'd God."
19. Kabir, *Songs of Kabir*, trans. R. Tagore, XVII.
20. Huston Smith, *Beyond the Post-Modern Mind*, pp. 111-112.
21. *King Lear*, ed. K. Muir, V.iii. 16-17.
22. Ibn 'Arabî, quoted by Corbin in *Alone with the Alone: Creative Imagination in the Sufism of Ibn 'Arabî*, pp. 174-175.

APPENDIX II: LONGING—THE FEMININE SIDE OF LOVE

1   "The source of my grief and loneliness is deep in my breast," trans. Charles Upton, *Doorkeeper of the Heart*, p. 34.
2. Farîd al-Dîn 'Attâr, *Muslim Saints and Mystics*, trans. A. J. Arberry, pp. 93-94.
3. Quoted by Louis Massignon, *The Passion of al-Hallâj*, vol. 3, p. 42.
4. St. John, 20:15-16.
5. Quoted by Chittick, *The Sufi Path of Love*, p. 241.
6. Hildegard von Bingen, quoted by Matthew Fox, *The Coming of the Cosmic Christ*, p. 37.
7. Quoted by Nicholson, *Studies in Islamic Mysticism*, p. 80. Al-Hallâj was executed for proclaiming *"anâ 'l-Haqq"* ("I am the Absolute Truth").

APPENDIX III: TWO WINGS TO FLY

1. *Mathnawî*, II, 1552f, trans. Camille and Kabir Helminski, *Rumi: Daylight*, p. 143.
2. See Vaughan-Lee, *Paradoxes of Love*, ch. 3, "Love and Violation," pp. 53-54: "This myth [the rape of Persephone] enacts the archetype of the maiden's initiation into womanhood, the dark rite of passage that is a transformation to a greater wholeness. When Kore returns from the underworld she is reunited with her mother into the single figure of Demeter-Kore, who is then symbolically joined by Hecate, the figure of intuitive feminine wisdom. Thus through her abduction, the innocent maiden becomes mother, maiden, and sybil all in one, embodying the three-fold nature of woman made whole."
3. *Mathnawî*, IV, 1357f., quoted by Schimmel, *I am Wind, You are Fire*, p. 71.
4. *Diwân*, "The Soul of the World," trans. R. A. Nicholson, *Rumi, Poet and Mystic*, pp. 182-183.
5. Quoted by Schimmel, *I am Wind, You are Fire: The Life and Work of Rumi*, p. 71.
6. *Mundaka-Upanishad*, *The Ten Principal Upanishads*, trans. Shree Purohit Swami and W. B. Yeats, p. 56.

7. "Tested by Fire and Spirit," video interview, 1988, from the DVD set *Branded by God*.
8. Lao Tsu, *Tao Te Ching*, trans. Stephen Mitchell, 1.
9. Quoted by R.S. Bhatnagar, *Dimensions of Classical Sufi Thought*, p. 144.
10. Katherine Haynes, *The Cosmic Web*, p. 59.
11. Yahyâ b. Mu'âdh, quoted by al-Qushayrî, *Principles of Sufism*, p. 290.
12. *The Book of Secrets*, ch. V, ll. 642-3.
13. Trans. N. Scott Johnson, "Ocean and Pearls, Ibn Sab'în and the Doctrine of Absolute Unity," *Sufism*, Issue 25, p. 29.
14. Trans. by Sara Sviri, *Fawâ'îh al-jamâl*, "Between Fear and Hope," *Jerusalem Studies for Arabic and Islam*, vol. 9, 1987, p. 349.
15. Sviri, p. 344.
16. Kalâbâdhî, quoted by Sviri, p. 346.

Glossary

Alchemy: the ancient attempt to create the Philosopher's Stone and mutable gold. In the West, mainly of Egyptian origin and Arabic elaboration, but also with Gnostic roots, especially in the idea that the World Soul was trapped in matter. Beginning with the *prima materia*, the alchemist heated, cooked, and washed the substance until it passed through the four stages of *nigredo, albedo, cinitritas,* and *rubedo* and became the Stone. In most texts, the basic idea was to divide up the four elements mixed up in the prime matter, refine and circulate them, and rejoin them in a *heirosgamos* or "chymical wedding" of opposites. Jung saw the *opus alchymicum*, the work of alchemy, as an unconscious projection of the process of individuation, which starts with an unconscious content (*prima materia*) and ends with the realization of the Self symbol (Philosopher's Stone).

Anima (Latin 'soul'): The unconscious feminine side of the man's psyche. She is personified in dreams by images of women ranging from prostitute and seductress to spiritual guide, Sophia (Wisdom). She can lead a man back to his soul.

Animus (Latin 'spirit'): The unconscious masculine side of a woman's psyche. He is the inner man who acts as the bridge between the woman's ego and her own creative resources in her unconscious. The animus personifies the *logos* principle. Through the animus a woman is able to express and manifest her true feminine self in the outer world.

Anima Mundi (Latin 'World Soul'): A pure ethereal spirit, which was proclaimed by some ancient philosophers to be diffused throughout all nature. It was thought to animate all matter in the same sense in which the soul was thought to animate the human. The idea originated with Plato and it also features in systems of Eastern philosophy in the Brahman-Atman of Hinduism. Subsequently the Stoics believed it to be the only vital force in the universe. It has been elaborated since the 1960s by Gaia theorists such as James Lovelock. It is the creative spirit in all of life.

Archetype: Irrepresentable in themselves, but their effects appear in consciousness as the archetypal images and ideas. These are universal patterns or motifs, which come from the collective unconscious and are the basic content of religions, mythologies, legends, and fairytales. They emerge in individuals through dreams and visions.

Atman: The individual soul or essence that is eternal, unchanging, and indistinguishable from the essence of the universe.

Coniunctio (Latin 'conjunction'): an alchemical operation that combines two chemicals to produce a third, different chemical. Psychologically, this corresponds to an unconscious experience (say, savage lust) which, combined with consciousness, becomes something different (healthy sexual desire). Jung identified the *coniunctio* as central to the inner alchemical process. It is often symbolized by a child born from the union of two parents. Wholeness requires a *coniunctio oppositorum* (conjunction of opposites).

Devas (Sanskrit 'divine'): one of many divine powers. On the higher levels they belong to the higher mental planes and are helping with the process of evolution. On the lower levels they are nature spirits which help in the process of creation.

Dhikr: A Sufi practice of the remembrance of God through the repetition of a sacred word or phrase. Done with the breath, either vocally or silently.

Gaia **Principle:** the understanding that the earth is a living being. *Gaia* is Greek for Earth, the Goddess of the earth. It also refers to a scientific hypothesis formulated by James Lovelock whereby all living matter on the earth is believed to be a single living organism.

Hadîth Qudsî (or Sacred *Hadîth*): are a sub-category of *hadîth*, which are sayings of the Prophet Muhammad. Muslims regard the *hadîth qudsî* as the words of God repeated by the Prophet Muhammad and recorded on the condition of an *isnad* (chain of verification by witness(es) who heard the Prophet Muhammad say the *hadîth*.

Indra's Net: a metaphor taken from the *Avatamsaka* (Flower Garland) *Sutra*, an important Mahayana Buddhist *sutra*. The *sutra* describes a vast net that reaches infinitely in all directions, and in the net are an infinite number of jewels. Each individual jewel reflects all of the other jewels, and the reflected jewels also reflect all of the other jewels. The metaphor illustrates the interpenetration and interconnectedness of all phenomena. Everything contains everything else. At the same time, each individual thing is not hindered by or confused with all the other individual things.

Inner Planes, Inner Worlds: subtle states of consciousness that transcend the known physical universe. The concept may be found in religious, metaphysical, and esoteric teachings, which propound the idea of a whole series of subtle planes or worlds or dimensions which, from a center, interpenetrate themselves and the physical planet in which we live, the solar systems, and all the physical structures of the universe. This interpenetration of planes creates a multidimensional universe with many different levels of consciousness.

Instinctual Wholeness: The natural wholeness that belongs to our instinctual nature, which, in today's culture, we appear to have lost and need to rediscover or reclaim.

***Lumen Dei* and *Lumen Naturae*:** C. G. Jung differentiated between two forms of spiritual light: *lumen dei*, the light proceeding from the spiritual realm of a transcendent God, and *lumen naturae*, the light hidden in matter and the forces of nature. The Divine Light may be experienced through revelation and spiritual practices that give us access to our transcendent self. The Light of Nature needs to be released through inner alchemy so that it can work creatively in the world.

Prana (Sanskrit 'breath'): the vital, life-sustaining force of living beings and vital energy, comparable to the Chinese notion of *Qi*. *Prana* is a central concept in Ayurveda and Yoga where it is believed to flow through a network of fine subtle channels called *nadis*. The *Pranamaya-kosha* is one of the five *Koshas* or "sheaths" of the *Atman*. *Prana* was first expounded in the Upanishads, where it is part of the worldly, physical realm, sustaining the body and the mother of thought and thus also of the mind. *Prana* suffuses all living forms but is not itself the *Atman* or individual soul.

Self: The archetype of wholeness and the regulating center of the personality. It is experienced as a transpersonal power, which transcends the ego, e.g., God.

Shadow: a psychological term introduced by C. G. Jung. The unconscious aspect of the ego which holds attitudes which are either unknown or rejected by the ego. Because it contains rejected or repressed elements of ourself it often appears as negative. Shadow qualities are not always negative, but may also be potentialities for which the ego has not taken responsibility. It is often the same gender as the ego.

Bibliography

Al-Qushayrî. *Principles of Sufism*. Trans. B. B. von Schlegell. Berkeley: Mizan Press, 1990.

'Attâr, Farîd ud-Dîn. *Muslim Saints and Mystics*. Trans. A. J. Arberry. London: Routledge & Kegan Paul, 1966.

Bakhtiar, Laleh. *Sufi: Expressions of the Mystic Quest*. London: Thames and Hudson, 1976.

Bhatnagar, R. S. *Dimensions of Classical Sufi Thought*. Delhi: Motilal Banarsidass, 1984.

Braden, Gregg. *The Mystery of 2012*. Boulder, CO: Sounds True, 2007.

Bruno, Giordano. *Cause, Principle and Unity*. Trans. by Jack Lindsay. New York: International Publishers, 1964.

Chittick, William C. *The Sufi Path of Love*. Albany: State University of New York Press, 1983.

—. *The Sufi Path of Knowledge*. Albany: State University of New York Press, 1989.

—. *Imaginal Worlds: Ibn al-'Arabî and the Problem of Religious Diversity*. Albany: State University of New York, 1994.

Corbin, Henry. *Creative Imagination in the Sûfism of Ibn 'Arabî*. Princeton: Princeton University Press, 1969.

Cummings, E. E. *Selected Poems 1923-1958*. London: Faber and Faber, 1960.

Donne, John. Ed. John Hayward. *Complete Poetry and Selected Prose*. London: The Nonesuch Press, 1972.

Eberly, John. *Al-Kimia: The Mystical Islamic Essence of the Sacred Art of Alchemy*. Hillsdale, NY: Sophia Perennis, 2004.

Edinger, Edward. *Anatomy of the Psyche*. La Salle, IL: Open Court, 1985.

Fideler, David. *The Soul of the Cosmos*. Unpublished manuscript.

Haynes, Catherine. *The Cosmic Web*. Ithaca: Cornell University, 1984.

Harvey, Andrew and Baring, Anne. *The Mystic Vision*. Alresford, Hants: Godsfield Press, 1995.

Housden, Roger. *The Fire in the Heart*. Shaftesbury: Element Books, 1990.

Jâmî. *Yusuf and Zulaikha*. Trans. David Pendlebury. London: Octagon Press, 1980.

Jensen, Ferne, ed. *C. G. Jung, Emma Jung and Toni Wolff: A Collection of Remembrances*. San Francisco: The Analytical Psychology Club of San Francisco, 1982.

Jung, C. G. *Collected Works*. London: Routledge & Kegan Paul.

—. *Memories, Dreams, Reflections*. London: Flamingo, 1983.

Kabir. *Songs of Kabir*. Trans. R. Tagore. New York: Samuel Weiser, 1915.
Keats, John. Ed. H. W. Garrod. *Poetical Works*. London: Oxford
　　University Press, 1956.
Kristeller, P. O. *The Philosophy of Marsilio Ficino*. New York: Columbia
　　University Press, 1943
Lao Tsu. *Tao Te Ching*. Trans. Gia-Fu Feng and Jane English. Aldershot:
　　Wildwood House Ltd., 1973.
——. *Tao Te Ching*. Trans. Stephen Mitchell. New York: Harper & Row,
　　1988.
Luke, Helen. *Woman: Earth and Spirit*. New York: Crossroad, 1986.
Massignon, Louis. Trans. Herbert Mason. *The Passion of al-Hallâj*.
　　Princeton: Princeton University Press, 1982
McLuhan, T. C. *Touch the Earth*. London: Garnstone Press, 1972.
Mitchell, Stephen, ed. *The Enlightened Heart*. New York: Harper
　　& Row, 1989.
Neumann, Eric. *The Origins and History of Consciousness*. New York:
　　Princeton University Press, 1970.
Newman, Barbara. *Sister of Wisdom: St. Hildegard's Theology of the
　　Feminine*. Berkeley: University of California Press, 1987.
Nicholson, R. A. *Studies in Islamic Mysticism*. Cambridge: Cambridge
　　University Press, 1921.
Nurbakhsh, J. *Sufi Symbolism*. London: Khaniqahi-Nimatullahi
　　Publications, 1984.
Plato. *Plato's Timaeus*. Trans. F. M. Cornford. Indianapolis: Bobbs-Merrill,
　　1959.
Rûmî. *Rumi, Poet and Mystic*. Trans. Nicholson, R. A. London: George
　　Allen and Unwin, 1950.
——. *Rumi Daylight*.Trans. Camille and Kabir Helminski. Putney, VT:
　　Threshold Books, 1990.
Schimmel, Annemarie. *I Am Wind, You Are Fire: The Life and Work of
　　Rumi*. Boston: Shambhala Publications, 1992.
Shabistarî, Mahmûd. *The Secret Rose Garden*. Trans. Florence Lederer.
　　Grand Rapids, MI: Phanes Press, 1987.
Shakespeare. *Hamlet*. Ed. by Harold Jenkins. London: Methuen & Co,
　　1982.
——. *King Lear*. Ed. Kenneth Muir. London: Methuen & Company, 1952.
Smith, Huston. *Beyond the Post Modern Mind*. New York: Harper
　　Colophon Books, 1977.
Sviri, Sara. "Between Fear and Hope, On the Coincidence of Opposites
　　in Islamic Mysticism," *Jerusalem Studies for Arabic and Islam*,
　　No. 9, 1987.

225

Tweedie, Irina. *Daughter of Fire: A Diary of a Spiritual Training with a Sufi Master*. Nevada City, CA: Blue Dolphin Publishing, 1986.
Vaughan-Lee, Llewellyn. *The Paradoxes of Love*. Inverness, 1996.
—. *Catching the Thread: Sufism, Dreamwork and Jungian Psychology*. Inverness, CA: The Golden Sufi Center, 1998.
—. *Working with Oneness*. Inverness, CA: The Golden Sufi Center, 2002.
—. *Spiritual Power: How It Works*. Inverness, CA: The Golden Sufi Center, 2005.
—. *Alchemy of Light: Working with the Primal Energies of Life*. Inverness, CA: The Golden Sufi Center, 2007.
Yeats, W. B. trans. (with Shree Purohit Swami). *The Ten Principal Upanishads*. London: Faber and Faber, 1937.

Index

G

Gaia Principle 123, 222
Ghalib (d. 1869) 106n
Ghazzalî, al (d. 1111) 102
global warming 5, 11, 90
Gnostics 99, 124, 221
Goddess xx, xxiii, 29, 32, 33,
    34, 50, 51, 178, 179, 185,
    186, 222
Gothic 99-100, 124-125, 139
grace 22, 130, 135, 144, 145,
    152, 186
Great Chain of Being 112
Great Mother 5, 6, 8, 32,
    65, 177-180, 186, 198,
    204-206, 209
guilt 205

H

hadîth 105, 222
hadîth qudsî 34, 222
Hâfiz (d. 1389) 176n, 218n
Hallâj, Mansur al- (d. 922) 192,
    195, 219
Hamlet 179-180
Heisenberg's Uncertainty
    Principle 216
Hermes Trismegistos 105, 111n,
    217
Hildegard von Bingen (d. 1179)
    xi, 3, 194n
Hopi 132
Hopkins, Gerard Manley
    (d. 1889) 105

I

Ibn 'Arabî (d. 1240) xix, 81, 112,
    182, 189-190n, 215

Indra's Net 58, 113, 222
Inquisition 134
instinctual knowing, instinctual
    knowledge 5, 12, 37,
    42, 84
instinctual self 11, 68, 103
instinctual wisdom 11, 59
interconnectedness 6, 11, 50, 57,
    93, 157, 222
Internet 6, 56, 58, 142, 164, 165,
    169, 216

J

Jâmî (d. 1492) 202, 215
Jesus 52, 193
Judaic tradition 31
Judeo-Christian 31, 179
Jung, Carl (d. 1961) 55, 101, 103,
    106, 114, 126-128, 142, 155,
    178, 181, 221, 222, 223

K

Kabir (d. ca 1518) 185n
Kali 136
Kalâbâdhî (d. 900 or 904) 212n
Keats, John (d. 1821) 176-177
King Lear 188
Kingsley, Peter 216
Kun! 22, 202, 210, 211, 215

L

latâ'if 140
Leonardo da Vinci (d. 1519)
    125, 126
Lilith 179
logos 4, 77, 221
Lord's Prayer, The 139
Luke, Helen (d. 1995) 215

Acknowledgments

For permission to use copyrighted material, the author gratefully wishes to acknowledge: Princeton University Press for Corbin, Henry, *Creative Imagination in the Sufism of Ibn Arabi*, © 1969 Princeton University Press, 1997 renewed PUP, reprinted by permission of Princeton University Press; the lines from "i thank You God for most this amazing", Copyright 1950, © 1978, 1991 by the Trustees for the E. E. Cummings Trust, Copyright © 1979 by George James Firmage, from *Complete Poems: 1904 - 1962* by E. E. Cummings, edited by George J. Firmage, used by permission of Liveright Publishing Corporation; *Muslim Saints and Mystics* by Farid al-Din Attar, translated by A. J. Arberry (Arkana, 1990) Copyright © A. J. Arberry, 1966, reproduced by permission of Penguin Books Limited; three lines ["Whoever can't see the whole.../... Tigris in every sip."] from *The Enlightened Heart: An Anthology of SacredPoetry*, edited by Stephen Mitchell, Copyright © 1989 Stephen Mitchell, reprinted by permission of HarperCollins Publishers; and first selection (1) from *Tao Te Ching by Lao Tzu, a New English Version, with Foreword and Notes*, by Stephen Mitchell, translation Copyright © 1988 by Stephen Mitchell, reprinted by permission of HarperCollins Publishers.

About the Author

LLEWELLYN VAUGHAN-LEE, Ph.D., is a Sufi teacher in the Naqshbandiyya-Mujaddidiyya Sufi Order. Born in London in 1953, he has followed the Naqshbandi Sufi path since he was nineteen. In 1991 he moved to Northern California and became the successor of Irina Tweedie, author of *Daughter of Fire: A Diary of a Spiritual Training with a Sufi Master*. In recent years the focus of his writing and teaching has been on spiritual responsibility in our present time of transition, and the emerging global consciousness of oneness (see www.workingwithoneness.org). He has also specialized in the area of dreamwork, integrating the ancient Sufi approach to dreams with the insights of modern psychology. Author of several books, Llewellyn lectures throughout the United States and Europe.

About the Publisher

THE GOLDEN SUFI CENTER publishes books, video, and audio on Sufism and mysticism. A California religious nonprofit corporation, it is dedicated to making the teachings of the Naqshbandi Sufi path available to all seekers. For further information about the activities and publications, please contact:

THE GOLDEN SUFI CENTER
P.O. Box 456
Point Reyes, CA 94956-0456
tel: 415-663-0100 · fax: 415-663-0103
info@goldensufi.org · www.goldensufi.org

The Golden Sufi Center® Publications

by IRINA TWEEDIE

DAUGHTER OF FIRE:
A Diary of a Spiritual Training with a Sufi Master

———

by LLEWELLYN VAUGHAN-LEE

THE RETURN OF THE FEMININE AND THE WORLD SOUL

ALCHEMY OF LIGHT:
Working with the Primal Energies of Life

AWAKENING THE WORLD:
A Global Dimension to Spiritual Practice

SPIRITUAL POWER: How It Works

MOSHKEL GOSHA:
A Story of Transformation

LIGHT OF ONENESS

WORKING WITH ONENESS

THE SIGNS OF GOD

LOVE IS A FIRE:
The Sufi's Mystical Journey Home

THE CIRCLE OF LOVE

CATCHING THE THREAD:
Sufism, Dreamwork, and Jungian Psychology

THE FACE BEFORE I WAS BORN:
A Spiritual Autobiography

THE PARADOXES OF LOVE

SUFISM, THE TRANSFORMATION OF THE HEART

IN THE COMPANY OF FRIENDS:
Dreamwork within a Sufi Group

THE BOND WITH THE BELOVED:
The Mystical Relationship of the Lover and the Beloved

⌒

edited by LLEWELLYN VAUGHAN-LEE
with biographical information by SARA SVIRI

TRAVELLING THE PATH OF LOVE:
Sayings of Sufi Masters

⌒

by PETER KINGSLEY

A STORY WAITING TO PIERCE YOU:
Mongolia, Tibet and the Destiny of the Western World

REALITY

IN THE DARK PLACES OF WISDOM

⌒

by SARA SVIRI

THE TASTE OF HIDDEN THINGS:
Images of the Sufi Path

⌒

by HILARY HART

THE UNKNOWN SHE:
Eight Faces of an Emerging Consciousness

⌒

The Role
of the Feminine and the
Reemergence of the World Soul

www.workingwithoneness.org/feminine.html

The feminine has a central part to play in the work of global healing and transformation. Her natural consciousness holds a deep understanding of the interconnections of life, how all the different parts relate together: how this awakening oneness can unfold. And every woman has in her spiritual centers the sacred substance of creation that is necessary for life's regeneration. Without the full participation of the feminine nothing new can be born.

A relationship to the feminine is also necessary for the reemergence of the *anima mundi*, the soul of the world. Buried by masculine consciousness, the world's soul is crying out for our attention. She has the ancient wisdom and understanding of life's oneness that we need if the world is to be redeemed.

Over the past two decades Llewellyn Vaughan-Lee has given different teachings on the feminine and the *anima mundi*. Additional resources, including free audio and video can be found online at the web address as above.

Endorsements

... continued from the front of the book ...

"Vaughan-Lee has listened deeply and transcribed for us so we can awaken to the true feminine, which so urgently needs to be understood and embodied at this time in human history."

—LAMA PALDEN, SUKHASIDDHI FOUNDATION, WWW.SUKHASIDDHI.ORG

"This beautiful book brought tears to my eyes.... If only a fraction of the women on our planet were to realize and put into practice what Llewellyn Vaughan-Lee teaches here, what a different and better world we would inhabit. His words articulate so powerfully the journey unique to women, and the one women must take if our world is to heal into a new reality. I know the deep yearning in the feminine soul to live out its potential.... This is a book capable of changing not only lives, but the world we live in. I cannot imagine a more powerful and timely book."

—ROBERTA GUILLORY, FOUNDER OF THE RED SHOES, A CENTER FOR PERSONAL AND SPIRITUAL GROWTH IN BATON ROUGE, LOUISIANA, DEVOTED TO THE SUPPORT AND EMPOWERMENT OF WOMEN SINCE 1999

"As I surrendered to the compelling rhythm of *The Return of the Feminine and the World Soul*, I felt something stirring deep within me. Within every kernel of Llewellyn Vaughan-Lee's wisdom there is a seed of new possibility... and another seed within and yet another. As a woman, I experienced a profound wave of relief to be finally seen and validated by the masculine for the ancient wisdom I have carried in my DNA. As one of the many beings of light called to service during this crucial time of global transformation, I found myself re-energized by this message of clarity and hope. And as a spiritual pilgrim on the path to oneness, I felt a deep relaxation as I glimpsed my place within an intricate yet profoundly simple sacred pattern. Yes! Now is the time to allow the healing energy of the divine feminine to lead humanity back into balance and wholeness."

—KATHLYN SCHAAF, CO-FOUNDER, GATHER THE WOMEN

"I am fascinated by the realm of the soul and how many windows there are into it. I am also fascinated by the various forms of clay that our mother earth offers us through which we can commune with her. To me, the contemplation of how grains of wheat, ground into powder that are turned into clay and then, miraculously, transform into loaves of bread is a wondrous, iconic journey. For this reason, I grasp and appreciate this deeply thoughtful message of Llewellyn Vaughan-Lee. He calls us all, each in our own way, to contemplate the Divine Feminine, to encounter the realm of Sophia, and thus discover the nature of our souls and Knowledge of the Truth that passes all understanding."

—PETER REINHART, AUTHOR OF *The Bread Baker's Apprentice* AND *Brother Juniper's Bread Book: Slow Rise as Method and Metaphor*

"*The Return of the Feminine and the World Soul* not only speaks of the feminine, but to the feminine. I found myself reading this book very slowly. Sometimes after only one or two lines, I would instinctively put the book down, be still and listen. The truth of Llewellyn Vaughan-Lee's words would resound in my body—a felt sense, which would vibrate down to my cells. I was taken to the essence of feminine knowing."

—DALE GENGE, FACULTY MEMBER, THE MARION WOODMAN FOUNDATION

"Attempting to express the beauty and magic of this book with words feels rather inauthentic and only skims the surface of what is a rich experience of the great warmth of connection. My words do not convey the deep feelings evoked—feelings that gently embraced me and opened up a dimension of receptivity, lightness and the very presence of the Feminine. I literally felt the sustaining nourishment of the energies of creation. All day I have been working in the masculine mode of getting things done and at the end of the day to melt my mind into the nurturing embrace of creation was nothing short of magical. I end up with nothing but gratefulness to Llewellyn Vaughan-Lee."

—NANCY ROOF, FOUNDING EDITOR, *Kosmos Journal*

"... a powerful reminder of the deeper knowledge and wisdom that operates in the world.... beautifully articulates that which in so many ways is so difficult to articulate. Vaughan-Lee's insight into the power of the feminine, the urgency of bringing her more firmly into the world, and the recognition of what is at stake if we do not embrace her, are powerful arguments for all of us to not only hear, but to assimilate into our work and daily practice.... The book yet again reminded me that it is only through a renewed understanding of life's wholeness that we will we be able to heal our planet and our world.... A necessary and important reminder to us all to listen and be open to this reality."

—ELLEN FRIEDMAN, EXECUTIVE VICE PRESIDENT, TIDES FOUNDATION

"The idea that the world may be a 'communion of subjects' rather than a mechanical 'collection of objects,' is still difficult for many members of the scientific community to accept. Our science is still deeply rooted in the mechanistic philosophies of the 16th and 17th centuries. However a growing number of innovative scientists and philosophers have begun to make a case for a more feminine, ecological view.... I suspect everyone interested in exploring how we must now learn to live in our new world, a world in which we know that 'everything is connected to everything else' will find something inspiring and productive in this book."

—FREDERICK KIRSCHENMANN, DISTINGUISHED FELLOW, LEOPOLD CENTER FOR SUSTAINABLE AGRICULTURE, AND PRESIDENT OF THE STONE BARNS CENTER FOR FOOD AND AGRICULTURE

"At this time, any healing will require accessing the creativity and the joy inherent in knowing that the birth of new images is possible. As Llewellyn Vaughan-Lee explains in *The Return of the Feminine and the World Soul*, the masculine and feminine are beginning to understand how to hold the tension necessary to create the space needed for this to occur. This book nurtures our ability to listen from within our hearts and restores the dignity and value of feminine wisdom, and points to what is possible when imagination leads."

—ELIZABETH SCHREIBER, M.A. AND SAND-PLAY THERAPIST

"This is a necessary book and a brave one. Rejecting the anger and blame that have marred so much feminist thought, Vaughan-Lee yet maintains that balance can only be restored in the world by the intervention of an active feminine spiritual energy.... Over and over, Vaughan-Lee has been forced to use words that once belonged to the sacred, but are now stained and degraded by their constant deployment in books written to help people to enhance their egos, bank balances, or their power over others. Yet its message is not diminished. Vaughan-Lee has set out to change the way we think."

—KERRY HARDIE, AUTHOR OF FOUR COLLECTIONS OF POETRY, INCLUDING *The Silence Came Close*, AND TWO NOVELS, INCLUDING *The Bird Woman*

"Spiritual teachers are common, great ones are few, and visionaries are rare. Here, the reader journeys on Vaughan-Lee's vision of the divine feminine principle, and the urgency for us to access the wisdom brought forth by it in order to bring healing to a world so deeply in need. Through his vision, we are able to access our own vision of how we, too, can participate in this healing.... Vaughan-Lee brings forth a perspective that is unique to someone who is both a scholar and mystic."

—MARIANA CAPLAN, PH.D., AUTHOR OF *Eyes Wide Open: Cultivating Discernment on the Spiritual Path* AND *Halfway Up the Mountain: the Error of Premature Claims to Enlightenment*

"This book is the work of an alchemist—a vitally important contribution to the Great Work of rescuing the human soul from the darkness that currently shrouds it. In this dangerous transitional time, where ignorance, confusion and cruelty abound, its theme of the need for us to recover and comprehend the Feminine is of absolute and urgent relevance. Few people are able to define and evoke the Feminine in the way that Llewellyn Vaughan-Lee does; in poetic and beautiful prose, he speaks directly from his soul to ours, acting as advocate for the longing of the *anima mundi*, the World Soul, to be welcomed once again into our lives and our culture. He knows that this is the time of humanity's awakening: each one of us participates in the mystery of the light hidden within us and within all nature that is being awakened. For exploring this mystery so directly and deeply and with such insight, he deserves our deepest gratitude. Women and men alike will welcome and treasure this book."

—ANNE BARING, CO-AUTHOR, *The Myth of the Goddess: Evolution of an Image* AND AUTHOR OF THE FORTHCOMING BOOK, *The Dream of the Cosmos: A Quest for the Soul,* WWW.ANNEBARING.COM